BLAKE. WORDSWORTH. RELIGION.

New Directions in Religion and Literature

Series Editors: Mark Knight, Roehampton University and Emma Mason, University of Warwick

This series aims to showcase new work at the forefront of religion and literature through short studies written by leading and rising scholars in the field. Books will pursue a variety of theoretical approaches as they engage with writing from different religious and literary traditions. Collectively, the series will offer a timely critical intervention to the interdisciplinary crossover between religion and literature, speaking to wider contemporary interests and mapping out new directions for the field in the early twenty-first century.

Titles in the series include:

The New Atheist Novel: Fiction, Philosophy and Polemic after 9/11
Arthur Bradley and Andrew Tate

Do the Gods Wear Capes? Spirituality, Fantasy, and Superheroes
Ben Saunders

BLAKE. WORDSWORTH. RELIGION.

JONATHAN ROBERTS

New Directions in Religion and Literature

continuum

Continuum International Publishing Group
The Tower Building   80 Maiden Lane
11 York Road   Suite 704
London SE1 7NX   New York, NY 10038

www.continuumbooks.com

British Library Cataloguing-in-Publication Data
A catalogue record for this book is available from the British Library.

ISBN: 978-0-8264-2502-7 (paperback)
       978-0-8264-2233-0 (hardcover)

Library of Congress Cataloging-in-Publication Data
Roberts, Jonathan, 1970-
Blake. Wordsworth. Religion. / Jonathan Roberts.
p. cm. – (New directions in religion and literature)
Includes bibliographical references and index.
ISBN: 978-0-8264-2502-7 (pbk.) –
ISBN: 978-0-8264-2233-0 (hardcover)
1. Blake, William, 1757–1827–Criticism and interpretation.
2. Blake, William, 1757–1827–Religion. 3. Wordsworth, William,
1770–1850–Criticism and interpretation. 4. Wordsworth, William,
1770–1850–Religion. 5. Religion in literature. I. Title. II. Series.

PR4148.R4R63 2010
821'.7–dc22
2010002274

Typeset by Newgen Imaging Systems Pvt Ltd, Chennai, India
Printed and bound in India by Replika Press Pvt Ltd

For Ying, in love

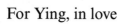

CONTENTS

Series Editors' Preface   viii

Note on Texts and Abbreviations   ix

Foreword by Christopher Rowland   xi

1 Introduction   1

2 Two Religious Visions   7

3 Biography and History   25

4 Autobiography   41

5 Mysticism and Psychedelics   49

6 Theology   67

7 Religion   81

8 In Conclusion   95

Acknowledgements   105

Notes   107

Bibliography   117

Index   125

SERIES EDITORS' PREFACE

This series of short monographs seeks to develop the long-established relationship between the disciplines of religion and literature. We posit that the two fields have always been intimately related, aesthetically, formally and theoretically, creating a reciprocal critical awareness framed by the relatively recent theo-literary thinking of figures such as Walter Benjamin, Martin Buber, Hans-Georg Gadamer and Geoffrey Hartman. Committed to reflecting on the question of how these two disciplines continue to interact, we are particularly concerned to redress the marked evasion of this relationship within existing scholarship. As Stanley Fish recently declared, religion has the capacity to 'succeed high theory and race, gender and class as the centre of intellectual energy in academe'. The books in this series are written by a group of critics eager to contribute to and read work intimate with both evolving and new religious and literary debates. Pursuing a variety of theoretical approaches to an array of literary and cultural texts, each study showcases new work on religion and literature while also speaking to wider contemporary concerns with politics, art and philosophy. In doing so, the books collectively map out new directions for the field in the early twenty-first century.

Mark Knight
Emma Mason

NOTE ON TEXTS AND ABBREVIATIONS

BR   Bentley, G. E, *Blake Records* 2nd edn (New Haven: Published for the Paul Mellon Centre for Studies in British Art by Yale University Press, 2004)

E   William Blake, *The Complete Poetry and Prose of William Blake*, ed. David V Erdman, Newly rev. edn (New York: Anchor Books, 1988)

WB   William Blake

'To Butts'   Blake's poem beginning 'To my Friend Butts I write' found in WB to Thomas Butts, Oct 2 1800 (*E* pp. 711–13)

Excursion   William Wordsworth, *The Excursion*, ed. Sally Bushell, James Butler, and Michael C. Jaye, The Cornell Wordsworth (Ithaca: Cornell University Press, 2008)

'Excursion'   Extract from Wordsworth's poem *The Excursion*, Book II, lines 764–916 in *Excursion*, pp. 99–103. For the sake of clarity, I have renumbered the lines of the two poems given in Chapter 2.

All biblical passages use the Authorized Version of the Bible.

FOREWORD

William Blake has as much to offer to theologians and philosophers as he does to literary critics. His work provides an astonishing engagement with the Bible, to which he is committed as 'the great code of art', and which he reclaims from all interpretations that would make it the instrument of tyranny and prescription. The significance of Blake's work is that he not only gives us distinctive *readings* of the Bible, but also offers us the opportunity to reflect on and rethink the act of interpretation itself in all its psychological, emotional, political, and interpersonal dimensions. Blake is one of the great exponents on the nature of interpretation or, as the matter is more formally known, hermeneutics.

The character of modern hermeneutics has been substantially shaped by the philosophical works of Hans-Georg Gadamer. Gadamer's 'philosophical hermeneutics' is the ground of the burgeoning fields of reception study and reception history, and these areas offer literary and biblical studies new possibilities for mutual reflection. It is at this juncture of literature, philosophy, and theology, that the present book is located. At the heart of Gadamer's hermeneutics is a critique of an over reliance on method, with particular reference to empiricism. Hermeneutics provides a critique of method rather than providing a method for enacting that critique. In the light of hermeneutics, the interpreter learns both to dwell within and to attempt to step outside the differing processes of interpretation. This process creates the critical space to discern better the nature of the interpretative space within which one is located. There is no formula to follow here, so the critic must innovate, working to find provisional, contingent, heuristic strategies in order to accomplish the hermeneutical task. In the case of the present work, this book stages the interplay of different interpretive paradigms in order to understand their commonality and possible grounds of dialogue.

Taking its cue from Blake himself, this study is made not in the abstract, but in relation to the specific and contested matter of claims to religious experience. The book asks how it is that we interpret and make judgments about other people's accounts of religious experience, and does so using two examples drawn from the writings of Blake and Wordsworth. The chapters that follow explore the ways in which those experiences might be addressed by a range of distinct interpretive paradigms that have governed the reception of these poets' works (history, biography, theology, and so on). In a culture that so often only seems able to endorse one paradigm by denigrating another, this book takes seriously Blake's aphorism 'without contraries is no progression' and resists mutually exclusive approaches by advocating instead a more complex, multifaceted dialogue that reflects our own human complexity. It is by allowing a democracy of paradigms that their potential for mutual enrichment becomes evident.

The conjunction of the literary, philosophical, historical, religious, and hermeneutical strands of this book is neither arbitrary nor coincidental. Quite the reverse: the book recognizes that the current state of affairs in which academic disciplines are by and large separate entities came about as the Enlightenment organization of knowledge began to push intellectual inquiry into discrete areas of expertise. Simultaneously, religious experience was becoming privatized, and occupying an increasingly compartmentalized place in individual and public life. This was the historical context in which Blake and Wordsworth were writing, fully sensible of the fissuring world around them, which Blake in particular resisted by seeking to persuade those who engage with his texts and images that imagination, 'poetic genius' and the 'spirit of prophecy' are the property of every honest person.

Like its poetic subjects and hermeneutical forbears, the book is not in the business of providing answers, but rather in opening out, developing, and stimulating the progress which comes through the dialectic between 'contraries'. The meaning of this text cannot be found in any individual chapter, but in the interrelationship of chapters both to each other, and to the whole. In this respect, the book asks to be read in a different way from most monographs. The hermeneutical circle set up in this book may be entered at any point. The linear progression of reading in this book is less a process of argument than the creation of an interpretative space which seeks to 'open the doors of perception'. It is an experiment in interdisciplinary engagement, attentive listening and dialogue between paradigms in which no one interpretive method trumps another.

Christopher Rowland
Dean Ireland Professor of the Exegesis of Holy Scripture
University of Oxford

CHAPTER 1

INTRODUCTION

Public discussion of religion in the UK and the US is characterized by conflict and acerbity. This is due in part to the antagonistic hermeneutical[1] structure of many contemporary debates: theism vs. atheism, creationism vs. evolution, heterosexual relationships vs. same-sex relationships, ordination vs. subordination of women and so on. This book looks to poetry for a different type of engagement with religion: one that can enrich rather than narrow understanding, include rather than exclude, and creatively interrelate – rather than destructively set at odds – different approaches to religion. Blake and Wordsworth achieve this inclusive form of engagement not from an unworldly perspective that has transcended such debates, but from attentively standing within them. As poets negotiating what might be termed inward and outward (or personal and corporate) experiences of religion, Blake and Wordsworth can help us to rethink our volatile public interpretive models.

What follows is a study of 'religion' in a Blake text and in a Wordsworth text, but it is equally a contemplation of the range of hermeneutical models available to those studying Blake and Wordsworth. To this end, 'religion' is an equal term in the book's title with 'Blake' and 'Wordsworth', and is not treated as a subset of Blake studies or Wordsworth studies. The book is, therefore, both explicitly a study of religion in a Blake and a Wordsworth text, and, implicitly, a reflection on how Blake's and Wordsworth's writing can help us to think about: (i) the nature of religion and religious experience today, (ii) how those phenomena might be communicated, and (iii) what happens when we describe them according to different interpretive paradigms. My aim is to indicate the diversity of these paradigms, their non-interchangeability, but also the enriched understanding they can provide when they are contemplated synoptically, rather than antagonistically.

My argument in this book concerns the processes of interpretation, and draws on the concept of the hermeneutical circle whereby the whole can only be understood in terms of the parts, and vice versa. We understand the character or nature of religious experience better through the contemplation offered by multiple methodological perspectives rather than through any single perspective, no matter how persuasive. This book can explore neither the 'whole' of religious experience in relation to Blake and Wordsworth, nor anything like all the 'parts', but within its limits it provides a 'whole' that exists in the interplay of a range of distinct and incompatible discourses. This much can be learnt from the poets themselves, as Blake's and Wordsworth's own religious narratives have many different facets: theological, psychological, social, biographical, historical, and so forth. When the two poets write about religion or religious experience, all these elements flow into one another, and the encounter with religion is not sectioned out by disciplinary paradigm. Academic study is inherently disciplinary, but the diversity of discourses that follow in the chapters of this book is intended to reflect the diversity of discourses to be found in dialogue within the poems themselves.

Literary critical monographs often provide a single, integrated methodological approach that is related to a range of poems or prose. The model in this book is almost the reverse: I consider only two short poems, but through a wide range of methodological approaches to them.

Mine is not a substitute for that other type of approach, but a companion to it. Research is often about ever-greater specialization, and that necessitates the focus of the more traditional monograph. I offer the present model as a means to step back, and also as a means to connect with wider (e.g. public) issues of twenty-first century religion, debates to which Wordsworth and Blake – in their complex and heartfelt responses to this subject – have something really important to contribute.

To achieve these goals, I have deployed an unusual approach in the writing of this book: chapter by chapter I present a range of different interpretive perspectives, many of which conflict with one another, and I do so without attempting to reconcile them systematically. In this discontinuity, as I will argue, these critical responses reflect the diverse life of the poetry under discussion. The conflict is not an analytical inadequacy that must be mastered: these poems are not – as human life is not, and religious experience is not – reducible to a set of well-ordered propositions. Rather, the insoluble diversity of critical approaches to these writers is a mark of their poetry's rich internal dialogue and hermeneutical plenitude.

Most of the approaches I adopt are recognizably academic, but because Blake and Wordsworth have a public image and influence that extends far beyond the academic sphere, I have also included non-scholarly voices, even when this inclusiveness means that some sections (particularly Chapter 4) are distinctly 'unacademic'. My hope is that the different methodologies that I present chapter by chapter will bring this diversity into focus without using any one approach to trump the others (the fact that some of the chapters get the last word on their predecessors is *not* an indication of the loyalties of the book at large, but is rather a side-effect of the fact that reading is a sequential experience). For this reason,

I attempt to identify with each of these positions, but not exclusively with any single one of them. I enact the identification by writing in the first person in the hope that voicing these positions enables them to interact, to criticize, and even to contradict each other, as they do in the poems. And, because I write in the first person, because 'I' narrate them, I thereby criticize and contradict myself, speaking at points as if I do not know my own motivations. This is a heuristic solution to a hermeneutical challenge, and I hope that the reader does not find it disingenuous.[2] Each chapter has, I think, something valuable to offer, and each presents problems. None is intended to be identical with my own voice, and I hope that I do not parody any of the positions that I take up: this is a danger given that I am only presenting shards of each approach, but in no case is what I have presented intended to represent the whole. The chapters are not arranged in an order of privilege, but I have begun with biography, as it brings the texts and contexts to the fore. As with any work of this sort, the critics I have drawn on exceed those whom I name in the text. A clearer picture of my resources is given in the bibliography.

The two texts I work with are Blake's poem 'To my friend Butts' and an extract from Wordsworth's *The Excursion* recounting a naturalized vision of the New Jerusalem. I chose these particular texts, first because I think they are great poems, and secondly because although they are both widely anthologized, there has been comparatively little critical work written on them. The two passages might be described as being both well-known and neglected. It is difficult to quantify 'neglect' in this context, but at the time of writing, there is no popular edition of *The Excursion* in print.[3] Nonetheless, the extract of the poem that I use (taken from Book II of the 1814 edition) is well known. The Blake text is perhaps less well known. Usually referred to by its first line 'To my friend Butts', it is a quite widely anthologized poem drawn from a letter to Blake's friend Thomas Butts in 1800 describing the poet's vision on the beach at Felpham. The poem is almost always abridged in anthologies, and, taken as a whole, has received little critical discussion. I think it deserves attention, as read together with the letter which contains it, it is one of his most important works, showing a different face from the angry prophet and unearthly mystic that often characterize depictions of Blake. Both texts are given in full in Chapter 2.

Given the range of perspectives in this book, I have wanted to maintain continuity by staying with the same literary texts throughout, and I have chosen texts for comparative purposes that share certain characteristics: both deal with a personal religious experience; both take place within an identifiable locale; in both cases the religious experience in question was also alluded to in a 'non-literary' context (diaries, letters); and both are moments of solitude in a natural setting.

I should stress at this point that the aim of this book is *not* to provide conclusive close readings of these poems. To do so would be to commit to the very foundationalism that this book is questioning. This book is intended to be, as it were, a companion to reading those poems and discerning what they offer on religion, but it is not intended to provide the reading (or religious experience) itself. The same applies to the relationship of this book to the critical approaches it engages with: I provide only partial and limited engagements, and my critical examples could have been indefinitely multiplied and extended. But to what end? Believing that the book could find stable solutions through such a process is again a kind of foundationalism: the belief that the answers are 'out there', and with just a little more time and a little more labour,

the world will reveal itself for what it is. This book offers
something different. Emulating the poems themselves,
it offers samples of life, not totalities, and moments of
religious response, but not 'religion' itself.

TWO RELIGIOUS VISIONS

This chapter provides narrative accounts of the two visionary poems with which this book is concerned. In each case, it provides an informal description of the setting and events of each poem, and these accounts are then followed by the poems themselves. The accounts are intended to provide an introduction to the poems, taking the poems on their own terms. I begin with the story of Blake's 1800 poem 'To my friend Butts'.

Look at the picture opposite. It is Blake's sketch of Felpham, the small coastal village where he and his wife Catherine lived from 1800–1803. Imagine that you beheld that same scene today, what would you see? If you stepped from a boat, from the English channel, and walked up Felpham sands tomorrow, the first thing you might notice is that the huge white windmill on the left has gone. That was demolished in 1879 after the sea eroded the coastline[1]; and that building in the centre of the picture – the round tower that looks something like a lighthouse rising between the trees – that's gone too. That was 'The Turret', home of the poet William Hayley, and the place where Blake worked, decorating the library, engraving, and printing during his stay in Felpham. It was demolished in 1961.

The sea from which you have stepped looks much the same now as then – on sunny days it is a wonderful turquoise colour at Felpham – but leaving that behind you, you would crunch your way up the shale of the lower shore, then onto a band of pebbles, before crossing the 1950s sea wall and promenade into 'Blake's Road' as you

'Landscape near Felpham', c. 1800, The Tate Gallery

head towards the village. The early twentieth-century tennis club would be on your left, and to your right, the mid-50s Felpham Sailing Club along with a row of painted council beach huts. Once over the prom, the road lies straight and level before you, but you can't see – as Blake would have seen – the medieval Church of St Mary in the distance (to the right of the windmill on the sketch) because of all the twentieth-century housing that now intervenes. Nonetheless, you can stay oriented with the sketch because by following the road, you'd be walking up that fence on the right of the picture, heading towards that cottage in the beam of sunlight. In 1800, and for the next three years, that was Blake's home. Keep going a little further and you'd reach *The Fox*, the pub built a year before the Blakes arrived in Felpham, and the scene of Blake's famous humiliation of the soldier John Scolfield.[2]

Blake's seventeenth-century cottage has now had the lime mortar knocked off to display the knapped flint walls, but in his day, it was mortared and whitewashed. You can see it illustrated so on plate 36 of his poem *Milton*, as well as in early twentieth-century photographs of the cottage. In Blake's picture, there's an angel in the sky over the garden, but now that's gone, and has been replaced by a high fence running along the side of the lawn to prevent tourists from peering in. When Blake lived here, skylarks nested on the open farmland (they turn up in *Milton* too), but their song has long disappeared, and in its place, the yelping and laughing of herring gulls.

What was Blake's life like in Felpham? We don't know from diaries, but we do have some of his correspondence from the period, and in particular an account of the events of 2nd October 1800 that Blake described in a letter to his friend and patron Thomas Butts. 2nd October was a special day for Blake, as it was on this date that he was caught up into heaven – not in death, but in transfiguration – and looked down on the village of Felpham from the bosom of God.

By 2nd October Blake, Catherine his wife, and his sister – also Catherine – had been in Felpham a little over a week. They were delighted with the village and the Cottage, as their letters make clear. Blake wrote to one friend:

> Felpham is a sweet place for Study. Because it is more Spiritual than London[;] Heaven opens here on all sides her golden Gates[,] her windows are not obstructed by vapours. . voices of Celestial inhabitants are more distinctly heard & their forms more distinctly seen & my Cottage is also a Shadow of their houses.[3]

And to another:

> Our Cottage is more beautiful than I thought it & also more convenient. For tho Small it is well proportiond & if I should ever build a Palace it would be only My Cottage Enlarged.[4]

Perhaps after a week there they had finished unpacking the 16 heavy boxes and portfolios full of prints that they had brought from London, and Blake had more time to explore their environs.

The weather had been wet, but the air was mild on that Thursday morning, and as Blake walked down the garden path and through the gate into the field, the sun, rising to his left, was streaming through the clouds. He walked across the ploughed field that had been golden corn when he'd visited Felpham two months earlier, but which was now cut to stubble. All before him across the open field lay the sea, turquoise and deep blue in the morning light as the clouds shifted over it. The tide was coming in, but was not yet high, and Blake walked over the rust and gray mix of pebbles that make up the upper shore, and sat looking out across the band of shale and golden sand onto the sea.

He watched the sunlight glittering on the water, and gilding the clouds – 'heaven's mountains' he calls them – and meditated on the forms of light itself: as jewels, as bright particles, as glorious beams. They glittered and shone before him, now seeming separate, now like fragments of eternity in constant flux. This was the beginning of Blake's vision and he watched in astonishment as the same light beams began to unfold themselves in their true forms, the shape of man, the human form divine. They did so by beckoning to Blake in his solitude, then telling him that all created nature is human: each grain of sand, every stone on the land, each rock and each hill, each fountain and rill, each herb and each tree, mountain, hill, earth, and sea, cloud, meteor, and star *are men*, seen from afar. Blake advanced into the light, absorbed by it, and now suddenly his vision was moved to a different plane, for he was no longer standing on the beach, but had, in Paul the Apostle's words, 'been caught up into heaven'. Blake was no longer looking out over the sea, or up at the sun, he was looking *down* at the village of Felpham which lay far below beneath his bright feet. There below him he could see his own mortal form, his own body – his 'shadow' – and the shadows of the two Catherines and of his friend Hayley. His vision continued to expand, and those jewels of light no longer appeared as separate men, but now glowed together as one man: Jesus. Lovingly and smiling, Jesus began to infold Blake's limbs in his beams of bright gold, purging away all his dross, the mire and clay of his nature, and in a mild voice explained that Blake had awoken 'from sleep on the sides of the Deep' (that is, the sea), and that the world that lay about him is Jesus' sheep fold, and that the loud sea and deep gulf are the guards of that fold. In time, Jesus' voice mildly faded, but Blake stayed in his transfigured state, and 'remained as a child'; and even after the voice faded, the vision stayed with him: the fractured worlds of his life's times and places came together before him, bathed in divine light, and as Blake puts it: 'all I ever had known before me bright shone'. It was an extraordinary vision.

Blake returned home to the cottage and wrote a letter to Butts. Butts had written to Blake a few days before sending some of his own verses. Blake replied thanking Butts for these, and excused himself for not having completed Butts's commissions, then wrote two poems of his own, the first describing his vision on the beach, the second greeting Mrs Butts, and blessing her in the language of fertility. This is the letter:

Felpham Octr 2d 1800

Friend of Religion & Order

I thank you for your very beautiful & encouraging Verses which I account a Crown of Laurels & I also thank you for your reprehension of follies by me fosterd. Your prediction will I hope be fulfilled in me. & in future I am the determined advocate of Religion & Humility the two bands of Society. Having been so full of the Business of Settling the sticks & feathers of my nest. I have not got any forwarder with the three Marys or with any other of your commissions but hope, now I have commenced a new life of industry to do credit to that new life by Improved Works: Recieve from me a return of verses such as Felpham produces by me tho not such as she produces by her Eldest Son. however such as they are. I cannot resist the temptation to send them to you

To my Friend Butts I write
My first Vision of Light
On the yellow sands sitting
The Sun was Emitting

His Glorious beams   5
From Heavens high Streams
Over Sea over Land
My Eyes did Expand
Into regions of air
Away from all Care   10
Into regions of fire
Remote from Desire
The Light of the Morning
Heavens Mountains adorning
In particles bright   15
The jewels of Light
Distinct shone & clear –
Amazd & in fear
I each particle gazed
Astonishd Amazed   20
For each was a Man
Human formd. Swift I ran
For they beckond to me
Remote by the Sea
Saying. Each grain of Sand   25
Every Stone on the Land
Each rock & each hill
Each fountain & rill
Each herb & each tree
Mountain hill Earth & Sea   30
Cloud Meteor & Star
Are Men Seen Afar
I stood in the Streams
Of Heavens bright beams
And Saw Felpham sweet   35
Beneath my bright feet
In soft Female charms
And in her fair arms
My Shadow I knew
And my wifes shadow too   40
And My Sister & Friend.

We like Infants descend
In our Shadows on Earth
Like a weak mortal birth
My Eyes more & more   45
Like a Sea without shore
Continue Expanding
The Heavens commanding
Till the jewels of Light
Heavenly Men beaming bright   50
Appeard as One Man
Who Complacent began
My limbs to infold
In his beams of bright gold
Like dross purgd away   55
All my mire & my clay
Soft consumd in delight
In his bosom sun bright
I remaind. Soft he smild
And I heard his voice Mild   60
Saying This is My Fold
O thou Ram hornd with gold
Who awakest from sleep
On the sides of the Deep
On the Mountains around   65
The roarings resound
Of the lion & wolf
The loud sea & deep gulf
These are guards of My Fold
O thou Ram hornd with gold   70
And the voice faded mild
I remaind as a Child
All I ever had known
Before me bright Shone
I saw you & your wife   75
By the fountains of Life
Such the Vision to me
Appeard on the Sea

Mr Butts will I hope Excuse my not having finishd the Portrait. I wait for less hurried moments. Our Cottage looks more & more beautiful. And tho the weather is wet, the Air is very Mild. much Milder than it was in London when we came away. Chichester is a very handsom City Seven miles from us we can get most Conveniences there. The Country is not so destitute of accomodations to our wants as I expected it would be We have had but little time for viewing the Country but what we have seen is Most Beautiful & the People are Genuine Saxons handsomer than the people [are] about London. Mrs Butts will Excuse the following lines

To Mrs Butts

Wife of the Friend of those I most revere.
Recieve this tribute from a Harp sincere
Go on in Virtuous Seed sowing on Mold
Of Human Vegetation & Behold
Your Harvest Springing to Eternal life
Parent of Youthful Minds & happy Wife
W B –
I am for Ever Yours

WILLIAM BLAKE[5]

* * *

Wordsworth's vision differs from Blake's, as it deals not with the voice of the poet, but with that of a character called 'the Solitary'. Wordsworth based the Solitary on a man named Joseph Fawcett, and it's his story that I recount here.

Joseph Fawcett was born of poor parents in a remote area of Scotland in the late 1750s. He distinguished himself in his youth through his intellectual precocity, and his family made a great effort to get him into the ministry. This plan succeeded, though not in a prestigious way, as Fawcett became chaplain to a military regiment. He fitted in well with the soldiers as he was socially adept and easy going, and his relationship with them was more that of a soldier among soldiers than that of a pastor to his flock.

The military life was shifting and uncertain, but Fawcett had the fortune to encounter – and the ability to win the hand of – an intelligent, wealthy, and remarkably beautiful woman. This change in commitments meant that he resigned his chaplaincy, and moved with his wife to a coastal cottage in a sunny bay of Devon. There the couple loved to walk on the Downs together through the fern and gorse, explore the wooded combes, and return to their cottage where myrtle flowered round the threshold among the holly and the yew. It was an idyllic life soon blessed with two lovely children, a boy and a girl. The family lived without close neighbours, and for seven years their lives seemed perfect.

Their happiness, however, did not last. Illness took the children and both died: first the sister, then the brother. The mother accepted her daughter's death as being the will of heaven, but Fawcett was unable to do so, and this difference in response severed the couple from one another. When their son died soon afterwards, the mother fell into an obscure gulf of silent grief and keen heart anguish, and within a year of the children's deaths, she too died.

The effect on Fawcett was devastating: he hoped for, prayed for death. He called for the spirits, and spoke to the grave, but no voice replied. His mind turned inward on itself, and he would most likely have sunk into a terminal depression had it not been for an unexpected event: in 1789 the Bastille fell, marking the commencement of the French Revolution. Though Fawcett had no connections with France and had never been there, he – like many others – saw in the Revolution the possibility of a new world, and swept along by revolutionary ideals he moved to London where he recommenced preaching with a reinvigorated emphasis on social justice. The Revolution offered Fawcett a means to overcome his grief, and consequently he made a total commitment to its cause: in a telling phrase he himself said that society had become his bride and its hopes his children. The blow, then, that Fawcett received when the Revolution turned into a reign of terror was immense. It was a kind of second bereavement so powerful that he lost his Christian faith, and left the clergy.

Disillusioned and desperate, Fawcett took ship for America in search of hope, but he carried his pain with him: on the voyage out he was haunted by the face of his lost wife on the deep. He arrived in Philadelphia, and from there travelled west into the New World in search of some sort of redemption or forgetting, but he found nothing but further disillusionment, and eventually returned to Britain, retiring to Westmoreland, in order to hide himself away among the hills. He moved to a cottage in Little Langdale, at the top of the Great Langdale Valley, near Blea Tarn, and sought to live out the remainder of his life in solitary existence in that remote place.

Though there were few neighbours in the Great Langdale valley, Fawcett knew a woman who lived at Patterdale. Her name was Ruth Jackson, a selfish woman according to Fawcett, and one who exploited an old Grasmere pauper who lived in the area. Jackson, in a way that ostensibly seemed hospitable, gave the old man food and shelter, but in truth, she provided a minimum of sustenance to him, and in return, she expected – and got – a maximum of labour.

Her poor treatment of this man came to a head on the morning she sent him – alone – up into the fells to dig turf for her fire. While he was at his labour, the weather turned, storms set in, and Ruth Jackson quickly began to realize not only that the old man might die, but that her reputation would be in tatters as a result. She panicked, and sought aid from Fawcett who, despite his anger with her, agreed to help. About this time, her husband returned home, and he and Fawcett set out in search of the old man, and before long they had found his abandoned tools. They shouted his name, but there was no reply. Darkness fell, the storm did not abate, and for their own safety they had to return home. Fawcett wept. The storm continued through the night, but in the morning the wind dropped and the rain abated, though the hills remained shrouded in an impenetrable mist. Fawcett and Jackson's husband gathered other men to their aid – shepherds from a neighbouring valley – and together they searched long and without hope. Close to giving up, they passed a ruin that had once been a chapel but was now little more than a wreck of stones. There, part buried under tufts of heath-plant they found the old man asleep. When they spoke to him, he was able to reply, but was bewildered and seemed unable to move. So the shepherds who had come to help in the search lifted him in their arms to carry him gently down the mountain. They began their descent through the mist, when Fawcett – who was following behind them – of a sudden experienced a mystical vision.

The essence of the vision was this: Fawcett stepped, suddenly, out of the mist into clear air, and saw the valley below him, full of the dark materials of the storm: clouds, mists, streams, watery rocks and emerald turf, each melting into each in the light. The appearance, however, was not that of a natural scene, but one of a mighty city, a wilderness of buildings, alabaster domes, silver spires, and blazing terraces. In the centre of the clouds that lay below him there stood a great throne with a canopy over it, the throne, perhaps, of God himself. Fawcett's heart swelled in his breast, and he cried out in response 'I have been dead, and now I live! But what am I living for?' He gazed long at the vision, which did not fade away, and eventually he descended the mountain alone.

As for the old man, he was returned safely to the village, and seemed at first to recover. This remission was, however, brief, and after three short weeks, he died. These, then, are the events in Book II of *The Excursion* that Wordsworth narrates. In the extract of the poem given below, the Solitary (who was modelled on Fawcett) is watching the funeral of the old man from a different part of the valley. As the scene unfolds, he recounts the story of these events to his visitors, beginning with the tale of the beggar – he whom 'our cottage has today relinquished' – and the old man's relationship with Ruth Jackson, the 'housewife' who exploited him:

> he, whom this our Cottage hath to-day
> Relinquished, was dependant for his bread
> Upon the laws of public charity.
> The Housewife, tempted by such slender gains
> As might from that occasion be distilled,   5
> Opened, as she before had done for me,
> Her doors to admit this homeless Pensioner;
> The portion gave of coarse but wholesome fare
> Which appetite required – a blind dull nook
> Such as she had – the *kennel* of his rest!   10
> This, in itself not ill, would yet have been
> Ill borne in earlier life; but his was now
> The still contentedness of seventy years.
> Calm did he sit beneath the wide-spread tree
> Of his old age; and yet less calm and meek,   15
> Winningly meek or venerably calm,
> Than slow and torpid; paying in this wise
> A penalty, if penalty it were,
> For spendthrift feats, excesses of his prime.
> I loved the Old Man, for I pitied him!   20
> A task it was, I own, to hold discourse
> With One so slow in gathering up his thoughts,

But he was a cheap pleasure to my eyes;
Mild, inoffensive, ready in *his* way,
And useful to his utmost power: and there   25
Our Housewife knew full well what she possess'd!
He was her Vassal of all labour, tilled
Her garden, from the pasture fetched her Kine;
And, one among the orderly array
Of Hay-makers, beneath the burning sun   30
Maintained his place; or heedfully pursued
His course, on errands bound, to other vales,
Leading sometimes an inexperienced Child
Too young for any profitable task.
So moved he like a Shadow that performed   35
Substantial service. Mark me now, and learn
For what reward! The Moon her monthly round
Hath not completed since our Dame, the Queen
Of this one cottage and this lonely dale,
Into my little sanctuary rushed,   40
Voice to a rueful treble humanized,
And features in deplorable dismay. –
I treat the matter lightly, but, alas!
It is most serious: from mid-noon the rain
Had fallen in torrents; all the mountain tops   45
Were hidden, and black vapours coursed their sides;
This had I seen, and saw; but, till she spake,
Was wholly ignorant that my ancient Friend,
Who at her bidding, early and alone,
Had clomb aloft to delve the moorland turf   50
For winter fuel, to his noontide meal
Came not, and now, perchance upon the Heights
Lay at the mercy of this raging storm.
'Inhuman!' – said I, 'was an Old Man's life
Not worth the trouble of a thought? – alas!   55
This notice comes too late.' With joy I saw
Her Husband enter – from a distant Vale.
We sallied forth together; found the tools
Which the neglected Veteran had dropped,

But through all quarters looked for him in vain.   60
We shouted – but no answer! Darkness fell
Without remission of the blast or shower,
And fears for our own safety drove us home.
I, who weep little, did, I will confess,
The moment I was seated here alone,   65
Honour my little Cell with some few tears
Which anger or resentment could not dry.
All night the storm endured; and, soon as help
Had been collected from the neighbouring Vale,
With morning we renewed our quest: the wind   70
Was fallen, the rain abated, but the hills
Lay shrouded in impenetrable mist;
And long and hopelessly we sought in vain:
Till, chancing by yon lofty ridge to pass
A heap of ruin, almost without walls   75
And wholly without roof (in ancient time
It was a Chapel, a small Edifice
In which the Peasants of these lonely Dells
For worship met upon that central height) –
Chancing to pass this wreck of stones, we there   80
Espied at last the Object of our search,
Couched in a nook, and seemingly alive.
It would have moved you, had you seen the guise
In which he occupied his chosen bed,
Lying full three parts buried among tufts   85
Of heath-plant, under and above him strewn,
To baffle, as he might, the watery storm:
And there we found him breathing peaceably,
Snug as a Child that hides itself in sport
Mid a green hay-cock in a sunny field.   90
We spake – he made reply, but would not stir
At our entreaty; less from want of power
Than apprehension and bewildering thoughts.
So was he lifted gently from the ground,
And with their freight the Shepherds homeward
    moved   95

Through the dull mist, I following – when a step,
A single step, that freed me from the skirts
Of the blind vapour, opened to my view
Glory beyond all glory ever seen
By waking sense or by the dreaming soul!   100
– Though I am conscious that no power of words
Can body forth, no hues of speech can paint
That gorgeous spectacle – too bright and fair
Even for remembrance; yet the attempt may give
Collateral interest to this homely Tale.   105
The Appearance, instantaneously disclosed,
Was of a mighty City – boldly say
A wilderness of building, sinking far
And self-withdrawn into a wondrous depth,
Far sinking into splendor – without end!   110
Fabric it seemed of diamond and of gold,
With alabaster domes, and silver spires,
And blazing terrace upon terrace high
Uplifted; here, serene pavilions bright,
In avenues disposed; there, towers begirt   115
With battlements that on their restless fronts
Bore stars – illumination of all gems!
By earthly nature had the effect been wrought
Upon the dark materials of the storm
Now pacified; on them, and on the coves   120
And mountain-steeps and summits, whereunto
The vapours had receded, taking there
Their station under a cerulean sky.
Oh, 'twas an unimaginable sight!
Clouds, mists, streams, watery rocks and
        emerald turf,   125
Clouds of all tincture, rocks and sapphire sky,
Confused, commingled, mutually inflamed,
Molten together, and composing thus,
Each lost in each, that marvellous array
Of temple, palace, citadel, and huge   130

Fantastic pomp of structure without name,
In fleecy folds voluminous, enwrapp'd.
Right in the midst, where interspace appeared
Of open court, an object like a throne
Beneath a shining canopy of state   135
Stood fixed; and fixed resemblances were seen
To implements of ordinary use,
But vast in size, in substance glorified;
Such as by Hebrew Prophets were beheld
In vision – forms uncouth of mightiest power,   140
For admiration and mysterious awe.
Below me was the earth; this little Vale
Lay low beneath my feet; 'twas visible –
I saw not, but I felt that it was there.
That which I saw was the revealed abode   145
Of Spirits in beatitude: my heart
Swelled in my breast. – 'I have been dead,' I cried,
'And now I live! Oh! wherefore do I live?'
And with that pang I prayed to be no more! –
– But I forget our Charge, as utterly   150
I then forgot him: – there I stood and gazed;
The apparition faded not away,
And I descended.[6]

CHAPTER 3

BIOGRAPHY AND HISTORY

The short biographical narratives given in the last chapter are based, in the first instance, on Blake's own account of his visionary experience in Felpham, and in the second instance, on information pertaining to the life of Joseph Fawcett, the individual on whom Wordsworth says he based the character of the Solitary in his long poem of 1814, *The Excursion*. Both accounts are supplemented by other records from the period.

The two short biographies are, at first glance at least, qualitatively different from one another, given that one describes the experiences of a real person (Blake), and the other, those of the blend of a fictional character ('the Solitary') and a real individual (Joseph Fawcett) on whom, to some extent, that character was based. That distinction between the ostensibly factual and the fictive has been important in the history of interpretation of these works. Readers and critics have been willing to treat a vision such as Blake's (which is recounted in a letter), as a crucial element within a larger biographical puzzle.[1] However, critics have tended not to draw on the dramatic narrative of *The Excursion* in the same way, choosing instead to turn to explicitly autobiographical poetry such as *The Prelude* as more appropriate source data for biographies of the poet. Critics and biographers have done this with due caution and sophistication, recognizing that they are dealing with Wordsworth's representation of his life, rather than simply the life itself, but nonetheless this difference in treatment (at least in the case of Wordsworth) seems centrally to do with different critical attitudes towards dramatic narratives and first-person lyric poetry. This is a particularly complex issue in the case of Romantic lyric poetry, given that its power derives in part from what seems to be a self-authenticating fusion of narrator and author: the 'I' of 'I wandered lonely as a cloud' is to be imagined as Wordsworth himself. One of my concerns in this chapter is the question of how we treat different types of literary resource when making judgments about the nature and authenticity of reported religious experience.

My general aim in this chapter is to say something about the reportage of religious experience, and to reach that goal I will go via some broader questions about writing histories, and more specifically, biographies. In particular, I wish to shed light on the key movement in the composition of biographies or histories whereby collections of facts (the empirical evidence) become – through concatenation – prose narratives such as those presented in the last chapter.

This chapter will be in two parts: first I will use the Wordsworth vision to reflect on whether we consider an autobiographical element to be the essential authenticating component of reported religious experience, and secondly, I will use the Blake vision to extend that question of authenticity to one of relevance: if 'authentic' corresponds to 'historical' in this context, then how do we set parameters on our historical data? How far do we pursue the details of our empirical resources, and how do we decide when to stop?

The special difficulty of discussing religious experience is its interiority: we depend on what individuals tell us about what took place for them, and we cannot verify it by other means. For this reason, there seems to be a necessary connection between religious experience and autobiography, and the validity of the former appears to be dependent upon the authenticity of the latter.

To put it another way, if individuals are willing to impro-
vise the facts about their *external* lives (as Wordsworth
does in *The Prelude*), how can we trust their accounts of
their *internal* lives? Put in these terms, the difficulty seems
fairly straightforward, but it is actually more complex
than it first appears. The complication lies in the assumption that – because of the explicit correspondence of
author and narrator – autobiography is a special, almost
extra-literary category of writing. But this assumption
may be erroneous: as Paul de Man demonstrates, autobiography is in fact a genre, which is to say an established
way of representing the world, and it is not a special
transparent mode of writing through which the truth can
almost reveal itself.[2] Without rehearsing his arguments
here, de Man makes it clear that it is disingenuous to
grant greater trust to a narrative simply because it is in
the first person rather than the third. This being the case,
when it comes to the reportage of religious experience,
a dramatized setting might be just as valid as an autobiographical one, and we might therefore have just the
same amount of validation of the religious vision of the
(fictional) Solitary in *The Excursion* as we do of the (autobiographical) Wordsworthian narrator of *The Prelude* or
'Tintern Abbey'.

The Prelude is no more or less 'literary' than *The
Excursion* – both are poems, yet *The Prelude's* appeal as
a source for autobiographical truth is not just that it
comprises a different type of content from Wordsworth's
other poetry (much is similar), but that it provides an
in-built autobiographical narrative frame through which
it makes sense of its own materials. *The Excursion* seems
less appealing in this regard because it adopts a dramatic
form, and the 'Wordsworth' character is only one of the
voices within the poem. But does genre *per se* either facil-
itate or impede the communication of religious experience?
Does a dramatic (rather than autobiographical) setting

count against the authenticity of the narrated experience? Probably not in the case of Wordsworth. After all, he was averse to communicating his fullest experiences immediately either in verse or correspondence, and he needed time to reflect on them: there were, for example, 14 or so years between the events (or rather non-events) at the Simplon pass, and Wordsworth's narrative account of them in *The Prelude*. Moreover, Wordsworth seems as content to work out his feelings regarding the deaths of his own infant children Catharine and Thomas through the character of the Solitary in *The Excursion*, as he is, say, to work out his feelings and experiences about Annette Vallon in the 'Vaudracour and Julia' section of *The Prelude*. Here, as in so many places, he appears to be willing to communicate something in poetry, that he would probably not put into a letter or into a diary. In Wordsworth's case at least, it seems that if we want biographical authentication of religious experience, we may have to include fictional biographies to get it.

This situation cannot, I would suggest, be simplified or resolved by focussing on the elements of the Solitary's story that can be shown to tally with Wordsworth's own experiences. Of course there are instances when we can do this: there *was* a man called Fawcett on whom the Solitary was, at least in part, based; there *was* an old man to whom these events happened – Dorothy describes him in her journal and Wordsworth said he was a Grasmere Pauper; and Ruth Jackson did exist, and her actions did lead to the death of that same man.[3] Of the vision itself, Wordsworth told Isabella Fenwick that the

glorious appearance disclosed above & among the mountains was described partly from what my friend Mr. Luff who then lived in Paterdale witnessed upon this melancholy occasion & partly from what Mary & I had seen in company with Sir G. & Lady Beaumont above Hartshope Hall in our way from Paterdale to Ambleside. (ibid.)

And then it is possible, of course, to trace the details of Mr Luff, the Hartshope walk and so on through letters and diaries in order to pin more precise dates and locations. Yet all of these factors may broaden our understanding without necessarily deepening it, as we are still left with the question of which of these biographies should be prioritized if we wish to better understand the vision itself: that of Fawcett, that of Luff, or that of Wordsworth?

Let us suppose, for example, that Luff had personally experienced a religious vision which Wordsworth had the imaginative facility to grasp in the fullness of its power, and the poetic ability to make available to others; then to whom does that vision 'belong'? This is one reason why *The Excursion* vision is so intriguing: what we have here is a compound experience of a number of different individuals: a close friend of Wordsworth (Luff), a stranger whom Wordsworth had heard about (Fawcett), an idealized narrative self (the Poet), an anti-heroic self projection (the Solitary), and so on. How does this impact upon our assessment of this passage as an authentic religious experience?

In terms of reported religious experience, *The Excursion* extract shows Wordsworth creating an aesthetically (and perhaps religiously) compelling vision based on a compound of the experiences of different individuals, and narrated through a tissue of dramatized voices. Yet despite this considerable literary complexity, this does not make the poem either more or less trustworthy as a religious text than the equally complex (though disingenuous) genre of autobiography. I wish to show this through comparison with the autobiographical instance offered by Blake: a text in a private letter, apparently directly

describing an intense religious experience that had happened that very day – surely as close as we can get to the
immediate transcription of a religious vision. I use the
rest of this chapter to think about some of the hidden
complexities of this case, and also to raise the question
of depth: once we have located what we consider to be
an authentic religious experience, how far do we press
the evidence? At what point do we draw a line and say
'enough'?

Biography is a kind of history, and the question of what
constitutes history has been a significant hermeneutical
debate, particularly since the advent of post-structuralism.[4]
The material of history seems plain enough: the extant
remnants of the past such as houses, maps, poems, letters,
mountains, and so on; and the translation of those facts
into narratives is so much part of our everyday thought
and conversation that it seems natural. However, that
translation conceals a hermeneutical question of how
exactly it is that we move from 'the facts' to an imagined
whole called 'the truth of the past' when there are in
fact, as Hayden White maintains, 'no stories in the past
to correspond to'.[5] That is to say, at the time of their
occurrence, events are not stories, they are only made
into stories at a later point. *The Prelude* is a story about
events, but is not itself one of those events.[6]

I wish to use the short biographical account of Blake's
poem given in the last chapter as a means to briefly open
out the hermeneutical relationship between fact and narrative. The facts in question include Blake's correspondence,
contemporary public records (such as nineteenth-century
maps), general information about the economy, geo-
graphy, and architecture of Felpham, and so on. The
narrative consists of an imaginary reconstruction of
one day in 1800 which blends these sources together to
form a plausible story. By avoiding any metafictional
elements, the narrative does not draw attention to its
own constructedness, but creates a textual space (via a

genre – biography) within which a religious experience can be described. To clarify the dependency of the religious experience on its narrative frame, I will now provide a brief chronicle of the same events that 'sticks to the facts' by only including sources that can be verified independently of Blake's letter. Interior (psychological / religious) experiences cannot be regarded as empirical data, so these have been omitted, making the account quite different. I have put sources in footnotes to keep the text readable.

2nd October was a full moon. There was a visible lunar eclipse that day that had been anticipated in *The Times* of the previous day.[7] At Felpham sunrise was 6.03am. Low water was 4.19am, high water, 10.54am.[8] The recent weather had been wet, but mild.[9] There was sunshine and some cloud cover.[10] There was a new resident in the parish, a 43-year-old man, stocky, Caucasian, balding, approximately 5 feet five inches, snub nosed, wide mouthed.[11] He was possibly wearing 'black knee breeches and buckles, black worsted stockings, thick shoes which tied, and a broad brimmed hat'.[12] He walks from his rented thatched[13] cottage, along a path through the stubbled cornfields[14] to the shore. It is morning.[15] The sun is shining on the channel. He sits down on the shale beach and looks out at the play of light on the sea.[16] Some time later he returns to his cottage. Possibly on the same day he writes a letter to his friend describing the experience.

How then does this account compare to the one given in Chapter 2? One might say that this is the more 'objective' account, but even here I have maintained a biographical focus of interest derived from Blake's own letter describing the events: it is Blake himself who has stimulated our interest in this time and place in relation to his own autobiographical narrative. It might therefore be more value-neutral to tabulate the data and to sort it chronologically:

Date	Time	Data / event	Source
		Blake stocky, Caucasian, balding, approximately 5 feet five inches	*BR* p. 390, though this description originally given by Gilchrist in 1863
		Blake wears 'black knee breeches and buckles, black worsted stockings, thick shoes which tied, and a broad brimmed hat.'	*BR* p. 389, though this description originally given by Gilchrist in 1863
1 Sept 1800		Blake's cottage about ¼ mile from the shore	WB to George Cumberland, Sept 1 1800 (*BR* pp. 95–96)
1 Sept 1800		Cornfields between Blake's cottage and the sea	WB to George Cumberland, Sept 1 1800 (*BR* pp. 95–96)
		'a sturdy two-storey thatched cottage of six rooms, for which he paid £20 a year to Mr Grinder, the landlord of the Fox Inn some fifty yards away.'	*BR* p. 746
23 Sept 1800		weather has been wet, but is now mild	WB to Butts, Oct 2 1800 (*E* p. 712)
2 Oct 1800		lunar eclipse	*The Times,* Oct 1 1800
2 Oct 1800	4.19am	low water at Felpham (0.6m)	http://easytide.ukho.gov.uk
2 Oct 1800	6.03am	sunrise	http://easytide.ukho.gov.uk
2 Oct 1800	morning	Blake sits on sand	'To Butts', 3
2 Oct 1800		sunshine and clouds	'To Butts', 4–5; 13
2 Oct 1800	10.54am	High water at Felpham (5.8m)	http://easytide.ukho.gov.uk
2 Oct 1800	5.39pm	sunset	http://easytide.ukho.gov.uk
2 Oct 1800		full moon	http://easytide.ukho.gov.uk

Tabulation may not be the answer however, as it still requires decisions to be made about whether to order the material by date of source, or by date of event, and to that degree it still retains an implicit narrative structure.[17] Is there a way round this? In order to eliminate a pre-conceived structure, the list of facts might be chopped up and scattered to the winds, but this would be to turn the list itself into the fragments of history that it was meant to represent. In this regard, 'history' seems to be a way of binding fragments of the past together, and is a sense-making narrative procedure. In these respects it is indistinguishable from the task of narrating religious experience, and this suggests that the former cannot ever satisfactorily underwrite the latter, as it does not have a foundational status: as narratives, history and vision are both in the same fix.

None of the discussion above is intended to question the value of history, or the possibility of histories being used to make right judgments (as in a court of law), or to testify to human suffering (as in accounts of war). Rather, it is intended to draw out the shared hermeneutical complexities of biography and autobiography, 'historical' and 'religious' experiences. In an academic culture in which the human sciences often seek to model themselves on the empirical methodology that is so successful in the natural sciences, there is a need for caution against the unreflective use of one sort of narrative project as a benchmark to assess another. History provides no simple solution to religion.

There is a second complication accompanying ordering and selection of evidence in assessing religious experience, which is the question of relevance. In particular, does an ever greater accumulation of historical detail necessarily add to our insight into these reported experiences? To address this matter I would like to return to the watercolour sketch by Blake mentioned at the beginning of the last chapter. It depicts a windmill, St Mary's church,

Hayley's turret, Blake's cottage, a field, and boats in the foreground. I am interested in the sketch because it was drawn on the beach at Felpham in the same place that Blake had his vision – and although the sketch itself is undated, the Tate Gallery suggests that it was circa 1800,[18] which would put it in the same year too. My question then is whether this might be a pictorial counterpart to the poem, and if so, whether it might provide more detailed empirical evidence to understand that vision. To my knowledge, no one has commented on this relationship between the poem and the sketch. Rather it has been taken that the picture is a straightforward, realistic exception to the imaginative visions that usually characterize Blake's work. Raymond Lister, for example, writes that the sketch 'amply demonstrates what the main body of his work has led some to doubt, that he was capable of painting straightforward landscapes', and adds that the 'realism of this watercolour perhaps indicates a cleansing of Blake's vision'.[19]

In order to think about whether this most unvisionary of Blake's pictures might be related to this most visionary of Blake's poems, I began with the question of Blake's position: where exactly was he when he drew the picture? Finding an answer to this was a time-consuming but practical matter: I was fortunate to have the help of a mathematician who created a piece of software that can triangulate positions from multiple landmarks and the distances between them, and was thereby able to calculate quite accurately where Blake was standing when he made the sketch. The results showed that Blake was some distance from the shore when he drew the picture, yet although the picture shows that there is some water (and a boat) between Blake and the land, there is not as much as one would expect: the shore seems too close. I checked this anomaly by using a different piece of software to collate, scale, and overlay early nineteenth-century maps of the area with present-day satellite images. This revealed that the shore has eroded substantially since 1800, and the area of ground on which the windmill once stood is now beach, and becomes submerged at full tide. Blake's sketch indicates that the tide must have been full at the time of composition for two reasons: first, the water on Blake's picture is lapping against the edge of a field on which a fence runs down to the sea, and secondly because Felpham beach has a considerable drop when the tide is out, of about five metres at the point where Blake stood, yet his eyeline is high, and looks slightly down on the view. Given that there were no buildings where he stood, the most likely explanation is that he was standing on a boat just off the now vanished moorings by the windmill.

What about the question of date? Given the optimism of the picture (such as the ray of sunshine falling on Blake's cottage) it seems unlikely that Blake painted it later in his stay when he became depressed at and about Felpham. So we might speculate that Blake painted it when his interest in Felpham was at its height, when he first arrived, and the Tate's suggestion of 1800 for the year seems right. What about the month? Well, the area was not used to grow timber, so the trees in the picture are presumably native deciduous hardwoods , and this is confirmed by their broad spreading shapes: they may be oaks. They are in full leaf, so the sketch was probably made between May and October. We can refine this further, because we know from Blake's correspondence that the fields between the cottage and the sea were corn fields. However, there is no corn visible in the sketch (e.g. around the fences), and the horse and rider seem to be riding through an open field. The corn would most probably have been cut in August, which would suggest that the sketch was made either in September or October. If so, can we narrow down the day?

Using astronomical software, it is possible to recreate sun, moon, and planetary positions for any location on earth, for any date in history. Although the sun is not visible on Blake's sketch, its beams are, and their convergence makes it clear where the sun was. Assuming the image is accurate, then given its elevation and position to the east, the sketch appears to have been made at about 11 am. This time is important because it enables us to work out the date, as we know we are looking for a day on which the tide was full at Felpham at 11am. There are only two such dates each month, and given that we have identified only two possible months in 1800, then there are approximately only four days on which this conjunction took place. One of the four is the date of the poem: 2nd October 1800. High tide that day was 10.54 am.

Are there any other reasons to think that this was the day on which the sketch was made? Yes. First we know from his letter that Blake was on the shore that day: he was in the right place at the right time;[20] and secondly, the weather conditions that Blake mentions in his poem (clouds with sunshine) also match what we see in the picture. All of this makes 2nd October a highly probable date for the scene, and there is every reason to believe that it is the counterpart of his vision in the letter to Butts: the tide, time, weather, sun's position, season, crops, trees, all match.

This correlation between the letter and the poem should perhaps not surprise us, after all, the combination of image and text is Blake's standard working method. Nonetheless, it is curious that this visual correlative to the poetic vision is so ordinary: Blake wasn't manipulating the scene, the sizes of the buildings and their relative positions are quite accurate.

Let us assume then that these inferences and conclusions are correct, and that we have a sketch made by Blake which has been verified as being made at the same time and place as the religious vision described in the poem. This must be a substantial piece of empirical data to add to our understanding of that vision. My question is, does it get us any closer to the religious experience itself? My answer is no, not if by 'closer' we mean that it has in some way diminished or simplified the hermeneutical task in hand. No quantity of empirical data could do that, although it might refine the interpretation. This material can be added to the table of data given earlier in this chapter, but perhaps it is more useful to extending the biography than to understanding the vision. Moreover, the 'results' it yields seem to have already been anticipated by the decision to accumulate this particular sort of data in the first place (via software, astronomy, triangulation, tide time tables, and so forth). This connects directly to the hermeneutical questions raised above by Rorty and White concerning the problem of joining up 'the facts': every decision contains an inclination, a hermeneutical trajectory, and those trajectories are influenced by all sorts of forces. What hasn't been done before? How have others approached similar questions? What interests me? What will be commended by my peers? What might gain funding?

Biography seems like a solid, foundational kind of literary criticism because of its empirical basis. Nonetheless, the solidity of the represented world is not, perhaps, due to the concrete quality of the facts so much as being a function of our mental engagement with the representation (the 'history') narrating those facts. The experience is like looking at a painting such as Georges-Pierre Seurat's *Sunday Afternoon on the Island of La Grande Jatte*, or Roy Lichtenstein's *M-Maybe*. Provided we maintain a proper distance, everything seems normal: bathers, a parasol, a woman, gloves, a world we recognize. But if we look closely, we see only dots, and if we look closer still, only the gaps between the dots. Historical reconstruction appears to take on the materiality of its sources, but the act of writing it, and even the act of perceiving it is hermeneutical: it requires the ability to see a pattern, not to look too closely, and only to look at the parts that are being pointed to. In this respect, history and biography are no different from any other genre, all of which require analogous (or identical) abilities to look in a certain way.

This trick of seeing is fundamental to the nature of narrative, and foregrounds the fact that the human organization of materials – rather than simply the materials themselves – may be a means not only through which we narrate and understand history, but through which, or in which, religious experience exists. Religious experience, like history and biography, may be a matter not so much of the facts, but of the organization of our experience of the world. The tabulation of facts earlier in this chapter showed that it is essential to have at least a minimal narrative element for religious experience to be communicated at all: without the 'inner' narratives, these accounts are no more than lists of assorted information. As lists of information they have their raison d'être removed because, of course, Blake and Wordsworth have created the narrative structure in the first place by writing these poems / letters. Without those records, we would have no reason to start rebuilding, nothing to go on.

It is important to note then that both Blake's and Wordsworth's poems are themselves 'histories', but they cannot be 'empirical' in any simple way. That is to say, Blake and Wordsworth have been engaged in the same act of writing histories, in so far as that process follows the model above – meaningfully connecting together 'facts' by narrative, whereby the connections between those facts (in the case of the visions themselves) are 'religious'. A view of a landscape, a grain of sand, these phenomena cannot be intrinsically religious. It is the organization and connection of these specifics – the narrative interpretive act – that is religious. This raises an interesting issue, because it suggests that even if the empirical elements are invented or copied, even if these experiences never happened, or even if they were delusions, they may still provide us with religious experience, whereby religion means a particular structure of engagement with the world. In the same way that, for example, a fictional role playing situation could provide trainee air crew or paramedics with ways of engaging with real life situations, so the value and meaningfulness of religious narrative may not depend on its empirical verifiability, but on the relationship it enables us to establish with our world.

CHAPTER 4

AUTOBIOGRAPHY

From its academic inception, literary studies has been anxious to appear rigorous, a 'proper' subject. It has shied away from accusations of subjectivity, and has been consequently inhospitable to personal testimonies. I offer my personal experience in this chapter in the hope that it might cast a different light on the question of Romantic religion, and may contribute to the illumination of that subject. Why might it achieve that? Because the matter of religion in Blake's and Wordsworth's writing is not translatable to a set of nested statements or alphabetical pigeon holes; it is not a poste restante awaiting the right archivist simply to unlock its treasures. The issue is more complex than that because while the more traditional modes of academic inquiry adopted elsewhere in this book can achieve a range of intellectual objectives, they are ontologically at odds with their subject matter when it comes to religious experience. When it comes to subjectivity, memory, and altered states of consciousness, approaching this subject through a personal contemplation may be more consistent with, and amenable to, the poems under discussion.

The experience I wish to describe took place within the course of a day, and can be recounted briefly. It occurred in the summer of 1993 when I was at the University of Lancaster in my first year of graduate research, studying Blake. 1993 was the year that Bill Clinton was inaugurated as US president; it was the year of the apocalyptic tragedy at Waco involving David Koresh and the Branch Davidians; and it was the year of the launch of the world wide web. In England, there had been late snow in May, but June was hot. After months of cool dull weather and rain, people were out in the sun – at least where I was – drinking lager at canal-side pubs.

The summer term had finished and I felt conflicted about my studies, as I wanted to connect to the lives of these texts in other ways than the cognitive or even the aesthetic. I'd read a lot of Wordsworth, and knew both the Butts poem and the *Excursion* extract through anthologies. Postgraduate study was keeping me in daily contact with these poets, but was also, I felt, pushing me away from them: after all, what did scholarship really offer as a way into the mystical human life that Blake invokes, or the mystical reciprocity with nature shown by Wordsworth? Whatever the enormous power of their poetry was for, I was pretty sure it wasn't –to borrow Blake – to take the forms of books and to be arranged in libraries.

I found those split feelings to be reflected in the reception of Blake's work. The whole question of the mystical side of his art seemed to be pre-eminent in the public idea of Blake, and simultaneously pretty much absent in the scholarship on him. Those few works that attempted to cross the divide – that is, to give some rationalized account of that mystical element in Blake – almost without exception ended up looking to psychoactive drugs as the closest experiential analogue. In particular, Aldous Huxley, one of Blake's great disciples, had denounced the social devastation and loss of life caused by alcohol and tobacco, while endorsing the pharmacological development of mescaline and related drugs that might offer individuals access to a higher world rather than simply the obliteration of the present one. More specifically Huxley argued that psychoactive drugs offer a transformation of the intellect and the senses of exactly the sort that Blake advocates in *The Marriage of Heaven and Hell*: that such drugs 'cleanse the doors of perception', providing an inner apocalypse and a new heaven and a new earth, and this could be brought about through a renewed personhood rather than violent social change.

It was at this time that Marshall, my flat mate's friend from the US, visited Lancaster, and brought in a film canister a gift of some peyote from his last stop, Amsterdam. Peyote is the common name of *Lophophora Williamsii*, a slightly bluish green cactus about the size and shape of a tangerine, that puts forth a single delicate flower from its centre, something like a daisy, but with pinkish silken petals. Though the living cactus is not subject to legislation, sliced and dried it has been, since 1971, a Class A drug, carrying a seven-year jail term for possession, due to its mescaline content. In the decades preceding this legislation, intellectuals such as Huxley had been free to experiment with psychedelic drugs, and even the British government was testing LSD on its own troops.

I didn't consume Marshall's gift at the time, but kept it until early August and then took it on a camping trip to the Lake District with a different friend, Mike. We camped in Hawkshead, and the day after arriving was clear sunshine, and we set out across the hills towards Windermere. It was a good walk out through open hill country and mossy woodland. We ate lunch on the shore of the lake, and watched the distant sailing boats gliding on the glittering water. We could see Bowness on the far shore, and its big white tour boats. As I knew it would be an hour or two before any effect, I took the prepared mescaline here, and we began the gentle walk back.

I knew there was likely to be some sickness and nausea, and there was, and although I felt anxious about this, we continued walking, and in time it passed, the sensation moving out from my head and torso, towards my extremities. After an hour or two we reached a beautiful tarn – a small mountain lake – from the shores of which, in the near distance below us we could see Hawkshead. We decided to spend the afternoon there. Mike lay on his back in the shade of some trees nearby, put his cricket hat over his face, and went to sleep. I sat on the edge of the path with my back leaning against a dry stone wall, and got my copy of Blake out of my bag.

After the nausea had reduced, a period of time passed in which little seemed to be happening. I had the Blake book on my lap – I wasn't even reading, my eye was idling over the lines in the Butts poem about how Blake's 'Eyes did Expand Into regions of air, Away from all Care Into regions of fire' – and it suddenly happened: I realized that the poem I'd read many times before was actually talking about my situation, the universe that I was in, and the living nature of every particle in it. This realization came on me like a flash, and was accompanied by a transformation in physical feeling from the nausea that had felt like a hole in my centre, to the sensation of a radiating core like a sun at the heart of my being, whose rays were slowly emanating out through my limbs.

The sensations from the mescaline had moved out now as far as my fingers, and I lifted them before my eyes and looked at a film of sand I had picked up on my hand, when I suddenly saw the exquisite beauty of every little grain of it; instead of being dull, I saw that each particle was made up on a perfect geometrical pattern, with sharp angles, from each of which a brilliant shaft of light was reflected, while each tiny crystal shone like a rainbow. The rays crossed and recrossed, making exquisite patterns of such beauty that they left me breathless. Then, suddenly, my consciousness was lighted up from within and I saw in a vivid way how the whole universe was made up of particles of material which, no matter how dull and lifeless they might seem, were nevertheless filled with this intense and vital beauty. It was the revelation that God was in front of my eyes – existence itself was God. What I was seeing was a visionary thing, it was a lightness in my body, my body suddenly felt *light*, and a sense of cosmic consciousness, vibrations, understanding, awe, and wonder and surprise. And it was a sudden awakening into a totally deeper real universe that I'd been existing in.

I knew with certainty now Thomas Traherne's meaning when he wrote

The Corn was Orient and Immortal Wheat which never should be reaped, nor was ever sown. I thought it had stood from Everlasting to Everlasting. The Dust and the Stones of the Street were as precious as Gold. The Gates were at first the end of the World, the Green Trees when I saw them first through the Gates Transported and Ravished me; their Sweetness and unusual Beauty made my heart to leap, and almost mad with Ecstasy, they were such strange and Wonderful Things.

All this, the feelings of connectedness, the sense of insight into forgotten things, the physical sensations, were new to me. But perhaps the strangest aspect of this experience was that I had no sense whatsoever of how long this went on for, I was conscious of moving in time, of things having no succession, and there being no absolute time, no absolute space, it being simply what we impose on the outside world. As a result, I remember that afternoon not as so many minutes spent by the side of the tarn interrupted by these strange excursions in time, but as years and years of heavenly bliss interrupted by short periods by the tarn. I would be withdrawn from my surroundings and from myself and have an experience, a state of euphoria, for a period of time that didn't end for me. It didn't last for minutes or hours but for months.

Seventeen years on, I have two peculiarly vivid memories from that day. The first was while we were still high on the hill looking down over Hawkshead. It's hard to record in words how it looked. The splendour of it was divine. It was the first earth, the earth that God had made. Hawkshead lay among hills rounded and softened by the light, preserved for eternity by the balminess of the day, the sweet haze of late afternoon, of midsummer, when nothing yet had begun to age or die. I cannot account for how long we remained there. It must have been some time, as my other acute recollection was of reaching the bottom of the vale at dusk, and wading through wild flowers of an uncut meadow. The air was still with the damp moisture of vegetation rising through it. The sun was behind the hills, but the sky was still light. It seemed that we walked through that field for ever, that we had reached the end of the earth. We came to the far side of this exquisite meadow and I heard insects below me, moths fluttering at my legs. I looked down, and the jeans that I was wearing were buttered with colour from the flowers, moist reds and butter cup yellows impasto on the creased fabric. We went back to the tent and lay on our backs in the grass watching the universe come out, and showers of shooting stars as the Perseids flashed overhead.

Ever since that experience of mescaline I have had a new, continuing visual appreciation of all art forms, an appreciation which I did not have before. Moreover, I have realized that quite literally everything is Self, everything in the whole field of experience – both what is usually known as self and all that usually is not self (people, objects, sky, earth, etc.). This Self which is everything is not the same as the ego-self. It is not that I, Jonathan Roberts, am everything, but that there is a more fundamental Self which is everything, including Jonathan Roberts. Since this realization, the mystical strand of Blake's and Wordsworth's poetry has a far clearer meaning to me than before. However, I cannot today do a better job of logically explaining Blake's visions than I could before. On the contrary, even now all logical arguments for or against Blake's and Wordsworth's visionary statements remain clearly beside the point.

CHAPTER 5

MYSTICISM AND PSYCHEDELICS

The last chapter is not scholarly, yet within the broader context of this book it may serve to bring into focus important questions about the nature and attainability of the experiences recounted in the Blake letter and the Wordsworth poem. Those experiences, it might be argued, typify the broader epiphanic character of the work of the two poets, which has traditionally been understood as being grounded in – in Blake's case – visions of God and angels, and – in Wordsworth's case – isolated epiphanies called 'spots of time'.

What I propose to do in this chapter to analyze Chapter 4 in service of developing this volume's broader discussion of Blake, Wordsworth, and religion. The way I shall do this is by: (i) tackling the question of mysticism – what is it, and what role does it play in the poems under discussion?, (ii) opening out the question of psychedelic drugs, their proximity to mysticism and their relationship to the two poets and, (iii) relating Chapter 4 to a history of popular and artistic responses to the mystical or visionary character of Blake's and Wordsworth's writings.

To begin with then, the question of mysticism. Numerous writers, including William James, Evelyn Underhill and W. T. Stace, have studied and sought to develop a taxonomy of mystical experience, and their definitions typically share key elements. Both James and Stace argue, for example, that mystical experiences have the common characteristics of 'ineffability', a 'noetic quality', 'transiency', and in James's case, 'passivity'.[1] In *The Varieties of Religious Experience* James doesn't discuss Blake (or Wordsworth, except in a footnote), but his account is helpful because it does not reduce mystical experience by collapsing religious experience into another discourse. James famously defines religion as 'the feelings, acts, and experiences of individual men in their solitude, so far as they apprehend themselves to stand in relation to whatever they may consider the divine',[2] and his emphasis on the quality of *experience* as a starting point (rather than any anterior explanation) is helpful in thinking about the nature of the religious experience communicated (or created) by Blake and Wordsworth.

One of the striking features of accounts of mystical experience is the numerous points of similarity that exist between such passages. These similarities – even across texts from quite different times and cultures – invite comparison, and there are broad similarities between the Blake and Wordsworth poems and many of the mystical experiences recounted by James. To take just one example, here is a passage that James quotes from J. Trevor's 1897 autobiography *My Quest for God*:

One brilliant Sunday morning, my wife and boys went to the Unitarian Chapel in Macclesfield. I felt it impossible to accompany them – as though to leave the sunshine on the hills, and go down there to the chapel, would be for the time an act of spiritual suicide. And I felt such need for new inspiration and expansion in my life. So, very reluctantly and sadly, I left my wife and boys to go down into the town, while I went further up into the hills with my stick and my dog. In the loveliness of the morning, and the beauty of the hills and valleys, I soon lost my sense of sadness and regret. For nearly an hour I walked along the road to the 'Cat and Fiddle,' and then returned. On the way back, suddenly, without warning, I felt that I was in Heaven – an inward state of peace and joy and assurance indescribably intense, accompanied with a sense of being bathed in a warm glow of light, as though the external condition had brought about the internal effect – a feeling of having passed beyond the body, though the scene around me stood out more clearly and as if nearer to me than before, by reason of the illumination in the midst of which I seemed to be placed. This deep emotion lasted, though with decreasing strength, until I reached home, and for some time after, only gradually passing away.[3]

There are numerous similarities between this passage and the Blake and Wordsworth poems. All three passages suggest what James calls a 'sudden realization of the immediate presence of God'[4] and all three confirm James's suggestion that certain aspects of nature 'seem to have a peculiar power of awakening such mystical moods'.[5] There are, moreover, many similarities in the imagery of the three passages (light, sunshine, hills and valleys); in their contexts (walking, looking, distance from and proximity to home / family, solitude, natural beauty); and in the experiential events (deep emotion, a sense of being in heaven, peace, a sudden and unanticipated revelation, clarity of vision, the experience only gradually passing away). In addition, there is in each case an emphasis on the disparity between ecclesiastical religion and authentic religious vision: Blake the narrator, the character of the Solitary, and J. Trevor are all figures who have at some time rejected the church or 'orthodoxy'.

These characteristics of Blake's and Wordsworth's writing have not been lost on later authors who have compiled anthologies and written studies of mysticism. Blake features substantially in Evelyn Underhill's *Mysticism: A Study in the Nature and Development of Man's Spiritual Consciousness* (1911), while Caroline F. E. Spurgeon in *Mysticism in English Literature* (1913) states that among English writers and poets 'the only two who fulfil this strict definition of a mystic are Wordsworth and Blake',[6] and both poets are quoted in F. C. Happold's *Mysticism: A Study and an Anthology*[7]. The mystical aspect of their work is also present throughout twentieth-century criticism of their writings. Jonathan Wordsworth writes of Wordsworth's 'mystical communion with the life force of the universe'[8], William A. Ulmer in *The Christian Wordsworth* discusses the 'One Life' that is 'a single vital energy permeating and ontologically underlying all natural creation'[9], while in *Romanticism and Transcendence*, J. Robert Barth describes Wordsworth's alpine epiphany as 'truly a mystical experience'.[10] J. G. Davies, meanwhile, dedicates a whole chapter of *The Theology of William Blake* to 'Blake and mysticism'. Even on its first publication, Henry Crabb Robinson wrote that Wordsworth's *The Excursion* was 'a poem of formidable size, and I fear too mystical to be popular'.[11]

Now, consider the other places in which the Blake poem has been quoted and anthologized, that is, outside the usual sort of poetry anthology. It appears in Nicholson and Lee's, *The Oxford Book of English Mystical Verse* (1917); in *William Blake, His Mysticism* by Maung Ba-Han (1917); in *William Blake in This World* by Harold Bruce (1925); in *The Protestant Mystics* by Anne Fremantle (1924); in John Diamond's *The Healing Power of Blake: A Distillation* (1998) and *Holism and Beyond: The Essence of Holistic Medicine* (2001); and in *Poetry for the Spirit: Poems of Universal Wisdom and Beauty* by Alan Jacobs (2002).

In terms of these particular poems, however, there is little scholarly analysis of their mystical character. There are a few short discussions, yes, but they tend to be grand on the claims, and short on the specifics. So for, S. Foster Damon the Felpham poem is 'Blake's clearest and most personal description of a mystical vision';[12] for Hazard

Adams the poem is 'the expression of an imaginative experience of the highest order';[13] following a discussion of the poem by Thomas Altizer[14], Blake is described as 'a mystical poet and seer, but in what sense remains unclear'[15]; and for David Wells the poem is 'a clear description of spiritual sensation'.[16] Blake's poem receives perhaps its fullest scholarly discussions in Leopold Damrosch Jr.'s excellent *Symbol and Truth in Blake's Myth*. Damrosch reads the poem as an account of a biographical event, and writes:

> In interpreting this deceptively simple poem, I think we need to take what it says with the utmost seriousness. It is not merely an extended metaphor intended to suggest that Blake feels imaginatively free at Felpham, but rather the fervent testimony of a visionary experience.[17]

Damrosch regards the poems to Butts as being unique in Blake's corpus, indeed as being 'precious because in them, as in no other surviving record, we hear Blake describing the immediacy of vision itself.'[18] Damrosch then goes on to discuss the character of this mystical experience, noting, as I have above, the correspondence to the accounts of Stace, Underhill, James, and Trevor.[19] He then expands his discussion in this way:

> What seems to be involved – although some religious writers resist the suggestion bitterly – is a physiological as well as spiritual phenomenon, which can be induced both by drugs and by ascetic discipline, and which some persons apparently experience spontaneously. A commentator on Plotinus notes that mysticism and psychedelic drugs both encourage 'abolition of the subject-object distinction and of the restrictions of space and time, and awareness of an animation

pervading even objects which common sense regards as lifeless.' Huxley said that under the influence of mescalin 'Visual impressions are greatly intensified and the eye recovers some of the perpetual innocence of childhood,' and an informant told Stace that mescalin did not 'produce' the sense that life shone through all things but only 'inhibited the inhibitions which had previously prevented him from seeing things as they really are.' Each of these formulations could serve as a direct commentary on Blake's vision of light.[20]

It is this more contentious relationship to psychedelic drugs and the history of interpretation of the two poets that I now turn to.

Both Blake and Wordsworth have – for poets – enormous numbers of admirers beyond the world of academe. It is unsurprising therefore that some of those admirers have wanted to experience first-hand the sorts of gestalts that these two poets depict, and have looked for ways in which this might be attained. Histories of mysticism suggest that such experiences are not easy to come by. In the tradition identified by, for example, F. C. Happold, such visions are the flowering of a larger religious life: Happold draws on the writings of, among others, the Blessed John Ruysbroeck, Thomas a Kempis, Walter Hilton, Julian of Norwich, Nicholas of Cusa, St Teresa of Avila, St John of the Cross, and so on. Individuals who lived a kind of monastic life or had a kind of religious tradition that is simply not available to most people today. Yet many individuals have claimed there is another way to attain these visions, a solution that – if the right vendor can be found – can be bought for the price of a book of poetry: the class of substances known as the psychedelics.

Psychedelic drugs have ancient connections with religion, perhaps even in the case of the Bible, as Dan Merkur has argued in *The Mystery of Manna: The Psychedelic Sacrament of the Bible*. Merkur sets out to demonstrate that manna, the miraculous bread of Exodus 16, given to the Israelites was, in fact, a psychedelic: the bread contained ergot, a naturally-occurring hallucinogenic grain fungus from which LSD is synthesized. The sacramental use of peyote by the Native American Church offers a contemporary example, and an instance in which the drug experience is not considered to be analogous to, but identical with the mystical experience.[21] The case for considering the two experiences as having a common core is strengthened by the fact that readers find reports of the effects of certain drugs to be indistinguishable from comparable reports of mystical religious experiences.[22] It is this proximity of the mystical and psychedelic experience that has led some individuals to argue that psychedelic drugs can offer the user a shortcut to paradise, bypassing all the discipline of life in a religious order. An early instance of such an argument is Thomas De Quincey's 1821 account of his first experience of opium:

I took it: – and in an hour – oh! Heavens! what a revulsion! what an upheaving, from its lowest depths, of inner spirit! what an apocalypse of the world within me! That my pains had vanished was now a trifle in my eyes: – this negative effect was swallowed up in the immensity of those positive effects which had opened before me – in the abyss of divine enjoyment thus suddenly revealed. Here was a panacea, a φαρμακον νἠπενθες for all human woes: here was the secret of happiness, about which philosophers had disputed for so many ages, at once discovered: happiness might now be bought for a penny, and carried in the waistcoat pocket: portable ecstacies might be had corked up in a pint bottle: and peace of mind could be sent down in gallons by the mail-coach.[23]

De Quincey is of fundamental importance to this discussion because, as Marcus Boon notes, his *Confessions of an English Opium Eater* are 'indisputably the first literary text devoted to drug use',[24] and comparable claims might be made for the poetry of his sometime friend Samuel Taylor Coleridge.[25] Moreover, Coleridge and De Quincey's drug use was not a historical aberration, but was consistent with the wider intellectual debates of the Romantic period. As Boon writes:

> Literary experimentation with drugs had its birth in the friendship between [Humphrey] Davy and Coleridge and the momentary possibility of a rapprochement between experimental chemistry, German Idealism, and Romantic poetics. [. . .] The philosophical dictum that 'the world is nothing but thoughts,' announced by Berkeley earlier in the eighteenth century, but systematized in various ways by Kant, Fichte, Schelling, and Hegel, became a lived experience for De Quincey and Coleridge in the dream worlds that opium and hashish opened up [. . .] The German Idealists themselves had little interest in this application of drugs. It was the British Romantics, empiricists at heart, who sought out experimental models for the study of the transcendental subject, whether it actually existed or not.[26]

However, the connection of drugs to Blake and Wordsworth is much more specific than simply sharing common ground with wider intellectual debates of the period. Blake, perhaps because of his epigrammatic dynamism or his psychedelic imagery, has, as we will see, been more extensively appropriated by psychedelic culture than Wordsworth, but it is of course Wordsworth whom De Quincey lives with, and it is the death of 3-year-old Catherine Wordsworth that contributes both to the character of the Solitary in *The Excursion*, and that precipitates De Quincey's descent into opium addiction. It is also Wordsworth who collaborates with Coleridge in *Lyrical Ballads*. It is easy to overlook or forget the fact that Wordsworth lived and collaborated with, in different periods of his life, both Coleridge and De Quincey, two of the most celebrated drug addicts of all time. My point is that Blake and Wordsworth are associated with drugs not due to taking them (as far as we know, they did not) but because of the mystical states of mind that their poems represent, and which from the outset drug users have recognized as familiar territory. It is telling, for example, that the religious vision from *The Excursion* discussed in this book makes its first cameo appearance in the first autobiography of a drug addict: De Quincey's *Confessions*. 'This passage', Alethea Hayter writes in *Opium and the Romantic Imagination*, 'haunted De Quincey all his life; he was forever quoting it'.[27]

That association between drugs and literature continued in the wake of the Romantics: Dickens, Barrett-Browning, Wilkie Collins, and many others used opium; Yeats took peyote in 1897, Walter Benjamin took mescaline in 1934; and Sartre took it intravenously in 1935.[28] The real flourishing of the psychedelics among intellectuals, however, occurred in the West in the 1950s and 60s when they were being investigated by governments and universities for their therapeutic properties (as well as possible military uses), and at a time when they were still legal. Their proliferation followed the discovery of LSD, first synthesized (and ingested) by the Swiss chemist Albert Hoffman in 1938. LSD has comparable, though not identical effects to mescaline (a psychoactive alkaloid naturally occurring in peyote, which may also be synthesized), and is comparable to other psychedelics including psilocybin ('magic') mushrooms, and Ayahuasca ('yage') an infusion prepared from a South American rainforest vine (*Banisteriopsis caapi*). These drugs are generally described as non-addictive; they affect brain functioning in ways that characteristically and dramatically alter sensory perception, and more curiously, the user's perceptions of time, space, and self. As Marcus Boon notes, in the early 1950s, 'both *Time* (1951) and *Newsweek* (1953) published articles on the use of mescaline in psychiatry, and the drug was in no sense a secret'.[29] The chief promulgators of that period were not pushers, but prominent intellectuals such as Aldous Huxley. Huxley, living in Los Angeles, was at the centre of events, and wrote *The Doors of Perception* about his mescaline experiences – a title taken, of course, from Blake's *The Marriage of Heaven and Hell*. Huxley was in contact with Humphry Osmond, sometime clinical director of a Saskatchewan mental hospital[30] and the man who coined the term 'psychedelic', from the Greek meaning 'mind manifesting'. Huxley subsequently became involved with Timothy Leary, who in 1960 'joined the faculty of Harvard University for a three-year appointment as Research Professor in its Centre for Personality Research'.[31]

The literary associations were by no means limited to Huxley. Among others they were championed by the Beat poets, and in particular their figurehead and self-professed inheritor of Blake's spirit, Allan Ginsberg. Ginsberg had taken peyote in 1956 while writing the second part of *Howl*;[32] he took LSD at the Mental Research Institute at Stanford University in 1959,[33] met Osmond in 1960, and through him, Timothy Leary. This was a culturally important connection because Ginsberg, as Boon puts it,

> opened his celebrity-filled address book to Leary, who continued with his program of experiments, both formal and informal. Among those who took psychedelics with Leary were Kerouac, [. . .] Neal Cassady; Dizzy Gillespie; Thelonius Monk; Franz Kline; Willem de Kooning; Robert Lowell; Arthur Koestler; Charles Olson; and Paul Bowles.[34]

In short, psychedelic drugs – before their legal pro-
scription – opened up a whole series of new possibilities
of understanding: as a stimulus to artistic creativity; as a
space for political opposition to the status quo; as a new
psychiatric tool for better understanding the mind; and
as a potential treatment for mental illness.[35] In these additional respects there are analogues to the 'Romantic'
interests and political sensibilities of Blake and Wordsworth (particularly in the latter's younger years). In short,
the literary credentials of the psychedelics are impeccable,
and the philosophical questions opened up by the psychedelics have much in common with those that preoccupy
writers in the Romantic period. The many readers who
have connected the world of psychedelics to the works
of Blake and Wordsworth have every justification for
doing so: philosophical, psychological, historical and
aesthetic.

I hope by this point to have shown that the histories
of mysticism and psychedelics are so entwined in the
reception of Blake's and Wordsworth's writings as to be
inseparable. This being the case, we are now in a position
to consider the meaning of the last chapter in relation
to the reception history of Blake's and Wordsworth's
works. First, what are the precedents in literary criticism
for the confessional mode adopted in Chapter 4? These
precedents are evident in criticism of the Romantic period
literature of the last three decades in which a number of
new historicist scholars have used a kind of confessional
self-dialogue to enable their books to discuss their own
limitations. For some readers this is an enlightening
critical self-consciousness, for others it is disingenuous
and frivolous.[36] Chapter 4 adopts such a mode but
provides the additional obstacle to the reader of sound-
ing like the voice of a conformist who wants to code as a
radical through recounting anecdotes of a rebellious past.
However, in an academic context, this sort of narrative is
counter-cultural in an additional sense: it commits to the

subjective, ineffable gestalts of mysticism (whether origin-
ating in religious training or the ingestion of psychedelics)
claiming that these are incommunicable in – and therefore formally antithetical to – the rational, cognitive world
of academic study. The sense of antagonism evident here
was also expressed explicitly by Huxley who, in *The Doors
of Perception*, wrote the following diatribe against the
scholarly community:

> In a world where education is predominantly verbal,
> highly educated people find it all but impossible to
> pay serious attention to anything but words and
> notions. There is always money for, there are always
> doctorates in, the learned foolery of research into what,
> for scholars, is the all-important problem: Who influ-
> enced whom to say what when? Even in this age of
> technology the verbal humanities are honoured. The
> non-verbal Humanities, the arts of being directly aware
> of the given facts of our existence, are almost com-
> pletely ignored. A catalogue, a bibliography, a definitive
> edition of a third-rate versifier's *ipsissima verba*, a
> stupendous index to end all indexes – any genuinely
> Alexandrian project is sure of approval and financial
> support. But when it comes to finding out how you
> and I, our children and grandchildren, may become
> more perceptive, more intensely aware of inward and
> outward reality, more open to the Spirit, less apt,
> by psychological malpractices, to make ourselves
> physically ill [. . .] no really respectable person in any
> really respectable university or church will do anything
> about it.[37]

Huxley's antagonism to scholarship is clear, but need
not be appropriated into the discussion of psychedelics
and mysticism. It is in fact possible to offer a critical
assessment of this kind of confessional writing without
seeking to either endorse or negate its world view. In the

case of Chapter 4, the narrative merits critical discussion for other reasons. First, its mix of confession and mysticism is not an aberration, but constitutes a central strand of the reception of both Blake's and Wordsworth's writing. Secondly, it foregrounds the relationship of the experiential and the autobiographical; and thirdly, it raises the question of authenticity because although it presents as a straighforward autobiographical account, the piece is demonstrably drawing – without acknowledgment – on a number of more or less well known sources relating to mystical experience and drug use, most of which connect in some way or other to Blake. After the introductory preamble and scene setting, the chapter is virtually all made up of passages taken from other sources. The paragraph beginning 'I had the Blake book on my lap' is drawn from Ginsberg in the *Paris Review*. The following paragraph ('the sensations from the mescaline') comes partly from Huxley's *Doors* (p. 60), partly again from Ginsberg. The paragraph after that, as stated, is from Thomas Traherne (*Centuries of Meditations*, p. 152), and the next paragraph ('All this, the feelings of connectedness') largely consists of quotes from Christopher Mayhew MP, being filmed under the influence of mescaline and describing its effects on camera for a BBC documentary entitled *Panorama*.[38] In addition to these specific sources, Chapter 4 in a more general way (imagery, tone, setting, and so on) is clearly modelled on both the Blake and Wordsworth poems, and on the J. Trevor narrative.

I will discuss the source of the final paragraph presently, but I wish at this point to linger a little over the Ginsberg narrative, not only because it forms the core of the Chapter 4 narrative, but because it epitomizes so much of the mystical and psychedelic history of responses to the two poets. The passage in question is Ginsberg's famous account (or rather accounts) of his vision of Blake. There is no definitive account of this experience, and the details seemed to change slightly every time Ginsberg recounted it, but the material here is drawn from a 1965 interview published in 1966 in the *Paris Review*, and reprinted in *On the Poetry of Allen Ginsberg*.[39] In brief, Ginsberg recounts the breakup of a relationship, feeling isolated, and sitting in his Harlem apartment reading Blake's 'Ah! Sun-Flower' and hearing Blake's voice – like the voice of the Ancient of Days – speaking to him, and presaging a mystical experience of the sort documented by James et al. This experience recurs while Ginsberg is reading 'The Sick Rose' and 'The Little Girl Lost'. It is quite a long, and not an entirely savoury narrative, which may suggest its authenticity or perhaps a desire to shock: certainly Ginsberg's claim that his consciousness had shifted is accompanied by what appears to be a (characteristic) total loss of social self-consciousness. He writes:

> About 1945 I got interested in Supreme Reality with a capital S and R. [. . .] So anyway – there I was in my bed in Harlem . . . jacking off. With my pants open, lying around on a bed by the window sill, looking out into the cornices of Harlem and the sky above. [. . .] As I often do, I had been jacking off while reading – I think it's probably a common phenomenon[.]

He then describes how he had been casually reading Blake's 'Ah, Sun-flower', when a change took place:

> Now, I began understanding it, the poem while looking at it, and suddenly, simultaneously with understanding it, heard a very deep earthen grave voice in the room, which I immediately assumed, I didn't think twice, was Blake's voice
>
> [. . .]

And my eye on the page, simultaneously the auditory hallucination, or whatever terminology here used, the apparitional voice, in the room, woke me further deep in my understanding of the poem, because the voice was so completely tender and beautifully . . . ancient. Like the voice of the Ancient of Days. But the peculiar quality of the voice was something unforgettable because it was like God had a human voice, with all the infinite tenderness and anciency and mortal gravity of a living Creator speaking to his son. "Where the Youth pined away with desire, / And the pale Virgin shrouded in snow, / Arise from their graves, and aspire / Where my Sun-flower wishes to go." Meaning that there *was a place*, there was a sweet golden clime, and the *sweet golden*, what was that . . . and simultaneous to the voice there was also an emotion, risen in my soul in response to the voice, and a sudden *visual* realization of the same awesome phenomena. That is to say, looking out at the window, through the window at the sky, suddenly it seemed that I saw into the depths of the universe, by looking simply into the ancient sky. The sky suddenly seemed very *ancient*. And this was the very ancient place that he was talking about, the sweet golden clime, I suddenly realized that *this* existence was *it*! And, that I was born in order to experience up to this very moment that I was having this experience, to realize what this was all about – in other words that this was the moment that I was born for. This initiation. Or this vision or this consciousness, of being alive unto myself, alive myself unto the Creator. As the son of the Creator – who loved me, I realized, or who responded to my desire, say. It was the same desire both ways.[40]

Ginsberg goes on to describe what he did next, how he visited his neighbours. There was, he says, 'a couple of girls living next door and I crawled out on the fire escape and tapped on their window and said, 'I've seen God!' and they *banged* the window shut. Oh, what tales I could have told them if they'd let me in!'[41] Ginsberg doesn't seem to think about why the girls might be frightened of a strange man besmirched with semen out on the fire escape, shouting about God, and trying to get into their room.

After the masturbation, the vision, and the Blake epiphany, Ginsberg describes the after effects, and recollecting these in tranquillity, steps effortlessly to a key mystical passage from Wordsworth's 'Tintern Abbey':

I *immediately* doubled my thinking process, quadrupled, and I was able to read almost any text and see all sorts of divine significance in it. And I think that week or that month I had to take an examination in John Stuart Mill. And instead of writing about his ideas I got completely hung up on his experience of reading – was it Wordsworth? Apparently the thing that got him back was an experience of nature that he received keyed off by reading Wordsworth, on 'sense sublime' or something. That's a very good description, that sense sublime of something far more deeply interfused, whose dwelling is the light of setting suns, and the round ocean, and the . . . the *living* air, did he say? The living air – see just that hand again – *and* in the heart of man. So I think this experience is characteristic of all high poetry. I mean that's the way I began seeing poetry as the communication of the particular experience – not just any experience but *this* experience.[42]

I dwell on this provocative, idiosyncratic narrative to make a point about the character of reported mystical experience. We tend to think of religious visions as being something extraordinary and unique, yet Chapter 4 shows that it is quite possible to take a central paragraph from such an odd anecdote as Ginsberg's, and to blend it with analogous accounts from two eighteenth-century poets, a nineteenth-century Unitarian minister, a twentieth-century novelist, and a twentieth-century politician, with their being no obvious tonal change. The oddness of this only really becomes apparent when one considers how much more difficult it would be to combine the more mundane aspects of the different narratives: the story of a respected labour politician tripping on mescaline administered by an old friend who now runs a psychiatric institute; an American poet-to-be nonchalantly masturbating while reading the *Songs*; a Victorian minister skipping church and going for a walk in the hills, and so on.

What then of the concluding paragraph of Chapter 4 (beginning 'ever since that experience of mescaline')? That is, in fact, lifted almost verbatim from a 1963 article entitled 'LSD and Mystical Experiences' by G. Ray Jordan published in the Oxford University Press *Journal of Bible and Religion*. The interchangeability of these passages is not only suggestive of the unity of the mystical / psychedelic experience, it is also suggestive of the extent to which what is academically acceptable is shaped by legal, social and political mores. While De Quincey and Coleridge are staple fare on undergraduate English degrees, it is difficult, at the present time, to imagine Oxford University Press publishing a scholarly article in which an academic states '[e]ver since my first LSD session I have had a new, continuing visual appreciation of all art forms, an appreciation which I did not have before'.[43]

To summarize this section: Chapter 4 offers a sort of survey of readerly responses to the mystical character of Blake's and Wordsworth's poetry. It does this by taking its cue from the anecdotal epiphanies of the poems themselves (of which the Felpham and *Excursion* passages are representative). By fusing the character of those passages with later response to those passages (and more generally with psychedelic-mystical narratives from a variety of sources), Chapter 4 draws out what is common to them. Moreover, by presenting this material in the first person, it maintains a trace of the aesthetic force of these experiences, and a sense of a new gestalt that must be encountered in its own terms. In addition, it is helpful in thinking further about the questions regarding the writing of history / biography raised in Chapter 3: as an autobiographical case study, it embodies the indecipherability of such accounts as the reader is left uncertain of its provenance. Is it knowingly manufactured from disparate sources? Or is it informed by sources read at some point in the past, perhaps half forgotten, but which have shaped and organized not only the experience itself, but also the recollection, and writerly transcription of that experience? These are questions applicable not only to such celebrated literary (alleged) drug visions as 'Kubla Khan', but also to Wordsworth's *Excursion* passage, and Blake's letter to Butts as well, and a 'yes' to either question would not invalidate these experiences given that these texts, like all literary texts, are both consciously and unconsciously intertextual.[44] Or, to put it another way, in conveying new religious gestalts via autobiography, narrative originality is not the precondition of authenticity.[45] In this context it may be the case, as Blake puts it, that the difference between a bad artist and a good one 'Is the Bad Artist Seems to Copy a Great Deal: The Good one Really Does Copy a Great Deal'.[46]

CHAPTER 6

THEOLOGY

Blake and Wordsworth are major literary figures who stand on the fringes of Christian orthodoxy, but who have nonetheless contributed to its enormously rich artistic heritage. This chapter offers a different perspective on religion in their poetry, looking to the Bible – rather than psychedelics or (as I will argue) a misconceived notion of mysticism – as the appropriate analogue for discussion. There are not only intellectual, but also moral reasons for this change of focus, not least that drugs destroy lives, and to suggest, as some of the earlier chapters do, that drugs and the experiences they provide are benevolent or beatific, is partial to the point of irresponsibility. Drugs cause and sustain wars, lead to violence, loss of life, and long-term physical, social, and psychological damage. Their distribution funds cartels that sustain a whole range of other forms of crime destructive to society. Anyone willing to turn a blind eye to this for their own transient pleasure should look into the histories of the mid-nineteenth century opium wars between Britain and China; into the bloody history of Pablo Escoba and the Colombian cocaine cartels; into the US invasion of Panama – 'Operation Just Cause' – in 1989; and into the current appalling combination of poverty, terrorism, and ongoing foreign military intervention in the world's current largest producer of opium, Afghanistan.

In addition to the human impact, the religious claims for drugs are troubled. The experiences that the psychedelics are reported to produce do indeed have a number of elements in common with reported mystical experience, but this by no means makes the two coeval, identical, or co-terminal. When the debate over religion and the psychedelics was at its height, two scholars of religion, R. C. Zaehner (sometime Spalding Professor of Eastern Religions and Ethics at Oxford University), and Huston Smith (sometime Thomas J. Watson Professor in Religion and Humanities at Syracuse University) looked deeply into this question, and each wrote extensively on the subject. Both men brought wide-ranging scholarship together with first-hand experience of their subject matter.

Zaehner set himself up as a forthright antagonist of Aldous Huxley and put the latter's claims for mescaline to the test empirically by taking the drug himself.[1] In the light of this experience he remained less than impressed with Huxley's assumptions, which Zaehner sets out as follows:

> In *The Doors of Perception* Mr. Huxley seemed to assume that preternatural experiences, conveniently described by the all-embracing term 'mysticism', must all be the same in essence, no matter whether they be the result of intensive ascetic training, of a prolonged course of Yoga techniques, or simply of the taking of drugs. In making these assumptions, of course, Mr. Huxley was doing nothing new. We have been told *ad nauseam* that mysticism is the highest expression of religion and that it appears in all ages and in all places in a more or less identical form, often in a religious milieu that would seem to be the reverse of propitious. (Zaehner, *MSP*, xi)

In other words, not only is the identification of the psychedelic experience and the mystical experience problematic, but mystical experience itself is simply not the homogeneous entity that Huxley suggests. Rather, as Leopold Damrosch Jr. neatly puts it,

> as a number of philosophers have recently shown, the search for a universal "core" of mystical experience has been a product of religious apologetics rather than of objective phenomenological inquiry. "Mysticism" is an arbitrary descriptive term rather than the name of a specific thing, and to ask whether Blake was a mystic is to expect a different sort of answer than to ask whether he was a mammal.[2]

For such reasons, Zaehner sets out to show that there are a whole series of category errors in the literature of drugs and mysticism, which not only collapse the different types of mystical experience, but also the distinction between mysticism and mental illness. Zaehner argues that 'if we accept the fatal "platitude", that not only can "mystical" experience be obtained artificially by the taking of drugs, it is also naturally present in the manic', then it must follow that 'the vision of God of the mystical saint is "one and the same" as the hallucination of the lunatic' unless 'the original "platitudinous" premiss is unsound'.[3]

It is for just this reason that Zaehner is impatient with Huston Smith's readiness to liken the drug experience to that of religious mysticism. Zaehner writes:

> Any comparison between drug-induced mystical experience and the religious mystical traditions is therefore bound to be extremely hazardous; for just as there are 'varieties of religious experience' and 'varieties of psychedelic experience', so there are 'varieties of mystical experience' [. . .]. It is, then, deplorable that a reputed authority on comparative religion and the history of religions, Professor Huston Smith of M.I.T.,

should be able to write with evident satisfaction that 'when the current philosophical authority on mysticism, W. T. Stace, was asked whether *the* drug experience is similar to *the* mystical experience, he answered, "It's not a matter of its being *similar* to mystical experience; it *is* mystical experience."'[4]

Zaehner may be right to criticize Smith on this particular point, but Smith is nonetheless a complex figure, and worthy of attention. He was a participant in, and exponent of, experimentation with psychedelics in the 1960s, but his use of psychedelics ceased with the end of the associated research programmes and Smith went on to explicitly contrast the life of the religious devotee with that of the drug user. In 1976 he published an article entitled 'Psychedelic theophanies and religious life' in which he critically discussed not the reality or otherwise of the psychedelic 'theophany', but rather its place within a larger religious life. Smith identified a number of particular problems with regard to this matter, and raised specific doubts over 'the staying power of psychedelic experiences':

> History shows that minority faiths are viable, but only when they are cradled in communities that are solid and structured enough to constitute what in effect are churches. To date, the psychedelic movement shows no signs of having within it the makings of such a church. Sporadic 'happenings' in makeshift quarters, and periodic gestures towards institutionalization, do not challenge this assertion; they confirm it by their ineffectiveness.[5]

Smith links the 'flawed social program'[6] of the contemporary drug culture to traditions of antinomianism, but perhaps more importantly to the fact that with no supporting church or community the drug experience becomes an end in itself, and this is unsustainable.

William James in *Varieties* similarly spends quite some time in his 'mysticism' chapter describing the historical tradition of 'methodical cultivation' of 'cosmic or mystic consciousness' 'as an element of the religious life'.[7] It is the willingness to believe that this faithful, longstanding, disciplined life context can simply be bypassed in the pursuit of instant mysticism that Zaehner finds most objectionable:

> in the past a man aspiring after a mystical experience was told with a singular unanimity that no such experience could be hoped for without a rigorous ascetic training lasting maybe several lifetimes. Now not many people are prepared to face these gruelling austerities, least of all the 'drop-out' young. But, Aldous Huxley has assured us, this was all quite out of date and needlessly tiresome and tiring: for what asceticism had done for the mystics of the past, drugs could do for the mystics of the present.[8]

What then are people actually gaining from their experience? Zaehner is scathing on this point:

> It is frequent and funny, if also unfortunate, to encounter young members of the Drug Movement who claim to have achieved a personal apotheosis when, in fact, their experience appears to have consisted mainly of depersonalization, dissociation, and similar phenomena. Such individuals seek their beatitude in regular drug-taking, continuing to avoid the fact that their psychedelic 'illumination' is not the sign of divine or cosmic approval they suppose it to be, but rather a flight from reality. Euphoria then may ensue as a result of the loss of all sense of responsibility; and this can

and often does lead to orgies of spiritual pride and self-indulgence by those who now see themselves as the inheritors of *It!*[9]

Assessing these matters is difficult, because although there are numerous popular anthologies of psychedelic / mystical experiences, there are few instances in which we are able to see the significance of a euphoric vision within a long-term autobiographical context. This is one reason why De Quincey is so interesting: his collected works provide the autobiographical records of a highly introspective and articulate drug addict, written over a period of half a century. Those records bear out the suspicions of Zaehner and Smith, as Michael E. Holstein has shown:

> To be sure opium had revealed to him [De Quincey] new dimensions of being, had favoured him with visions into the sacred mysteries of existence, but it had also paralysed his will to comply with the demands of a now sacred universe more complex than could be measured by canons of ordinary social intercourse or religious practice.[10]

De Quincey may have been emancipated in the short term by drugs, but in the long term, they paralyzed him. He is a helpful test case for other reasons too. One of the alleged liberations of the psychedelic epiphany is the sensation of being disconnected from linear time. One can actually see an individual undergoing this experience in the *Panorama* documentary mentioned in the last chapter. It is quite clear from his conversation under mescaline that Christopher Mayhew is experiencing a temporal disorientation whereby he senses being both in and out of time. This might seem like liberation in the short term, but it is less glamorous when it becomes clear that in a longer term biographical context De Quincey loses his ability to maintain any chronological order over his own mind, life, or experiences. As Holstein puts it:

> Once De Quincey is introduced to opium, the drug experiences and his subsequent dreaming conspire to diminish the importance of sequential time, for they employ contiguity, simultaneity, and temporal distortion to communicate their effects. Moreover, the mystical associations that the drug has for him suggest a higher order of meaning than the literal unfolding of events in time. Thus after his wanderings and with his initiation to opium, the *Confessions* ceases to rely on horizontal or sequential order and instead struggles to evolve a vertical or interpretive dimension as the order of meaning replaces the order of time.[11]

De Quincey's experiences would suggest that the collapse of time is far from being a self-evident good, but means, first, a collapse into his own pathology, and perpetual revisitation by the same torments and demons; and secondly, the collapse of any possible linear scheme of salvation: without time, De Quincey cannot live or act in the hope of future redemption; he is lost in an eternal purgatory.[12] The agonized records of Coleridge's and De Quincey's psychological and physical lives make it quite plain that whatever the source of the psychedelic epiphany, is also the source of the psychedelic nightmare: horrors lurk amid the paradises; there are hells as well as heavens, and to ignore the former out of simple preference for the latter (by, for example, presenting 'bad trips' as an aberration of an intrinsically benign experience) is a kind of deception.[13]

I hope I have provided a useful overview of why any interrelating of drugs to Blake's and Wordsworth's poems requires the utmost caution. It is also, I hope, helpful in disentangling these poets from a knot that has twisted around the previous chapters in this volume, viz., the idea that they were 'mystics'. The mystical credentials of Wordsworth and Blake are unclear, given that neither of them underwent what Zaehner calls 'rigorous ascetic training'. I follow Zaehner here who writes of the two poets:

> [In Wordsworth's 'Tintern Abbey'] there is an intimation, if you like, of something which transcends and informs transient Nature, but it is no more than an intimation. It amounts to little more than that there is a Spirit somewhere which pervades all Nature. There is no trace of an actual experience at all, either of union with Nature or communion with God. There is a dim perception only that there is a unifying principle in the universe. On these grounds Wordsworth can scarcely be classed as a mystic since, to judge from his writings, he does not seem to have had a 'unitive' experience of any of the types we have discussed. [. . .] Similarly, according to this definition, it is difficult to see how Blake fits in. Blake was rather a seer in the literal sense of the word: he lived in a world in which angels, prophets, patriarchs, demons, and even fairies were more real tha[n] the everyday life around him with which alone most of us are familiar. Though superb both as a poet and as a painter, he cannot be strictly classed as a mystic.[14]

As the last chapter showed, both the poem to Butts and *The Excursion* extract have continuously been appropriated in anthologies of mysticism by those of a syncretistic persuasion. This extraction and anthologization of these poems is itself interesting because there is a valid analogy to be drawn between, say, the piecemeal use of *The Excursion* to provide a mystical experience (to the reader of such anthologies), and the piecemeal use of drugs for the same purpose (i.e. for instant mysticism rather than as part of a life of true religious observance). None of this, however, is a criticism of Blake and Wordsworth themselves, but rather an observation regarding the histories of the interpretation of their works. Moreover, not all critics have attempted to reduce their textually complex religious visions to a single mystical strand. Blake and Wordsworth are, as some critics have shown, the authors of poems that are able to contemplate the character – and limitations – of individual religious visions by drawing on a democratic, common, one might say 'catholic' language of religious experience, and more particularly the Bible, to make that questioning possible. In other words, Blake's and Wordsworth's religious meditations endure, not because they have keyed into some universal transcendent plane and reported back via poetry; but rather because the public language of the Judaeo-Christian tradition has given them words with which to speak, and forms with which to communicate to other people in other places and at other times. To put this in Zaehner's terms, the individual religious experience can only occur as the flowering of the communal religious experience, even when it is at odds with that wider community, and even when the sense of community may be linguistic rather than liturgical.

There has been a range of important studies of the two writers in relation to Christianity. To name just a few, J. G. Davies and William J. Ulmer offer more traditional Christian theological frameworks within which to think about, respectively, Blake and Wordsworth. David P. Haney has provided a theoretically-inflected study of Wordsworth, while Thomas Altizer offers a counterpart for Blake. On a different tack again, Deanne Westbrook has looked in detail at the presence of biblical language in Wordsworth's poetry, and the discussion that will now follow is closest to that last work. The aim of the remainder of this chapter is simply to say something about the range of biblical and religious images and words that inform and sustain the two poems, and to point out that the poems can still be religious without being mystical, and can be read as textual, biblical, Judaeo-Christian epiphanies. The reason for making this argument is to offer a response to the vague public concepts of religion that have found their way into Blake and Wordsworth scholarship, of which 'mysticism' – as discussed above – is one example. A wider-ranging cultural misappropriation of 'mysticism' has enabled shifting and rather confused conceptions of religion to influence the interpretation of these poems over a long period of time. By looking at the matter of biblical allusion within these works, the critical conversation is shifted from the gesturally 'religious' to the biblically specific.

There are numerous minor allusions to the biblical text in both poems. To take one example from the poem to Butts, the shepherd (l. 63), the lion (l. 68), and the wolf (l. 68) all have multiple correspondences in the Bible, and their conjunction here seems to invoke the mountain of the Lord depicted in Isaiah 11. There, the lion and wolf appear together in relation to the lamb (Isaiah 11:1–6), a passage which in the Christian tradition anticipates the righteous figure of Christ bringing justice to the poor. The mountain and streams and sea echoed in Blake's vision (ll. 66, 6, 65) are also here:

> [W]ith righteousness shall he judge the poor, and reprove with equity for the meek of the earth: and he shall smite the earth: with the rod of his mouth, and with the breath of his lips shall he slay the wicked. And righteousness shall be the girdle of his loins, and faithfulness the girdle of his reins. The wolf also shall dwell with the lamb, and the leopard shall lie down with the kid; and the calf and the young lion and the fatling together; and a little child shall lead them. [. . .] They shall not hurt nor destroy in all my holy mountain: for the earth shall be full

of the knowledge of the LORD, as the waters cover the sea.[15]

Hearing the prophetic Hebrew text in the background takes us closer to the kind of vision that Blake is communicating: it is not, as it might at first appear, just a kind of ravishing of the senses, or a personal spiritual trip, but rather – as an experience of the divine – it is textually grounded in a biblical vision of human peace and equality. Both the Blake and the Wordsworth poems are organized around larger biblical tropes – in particular those of transfiguration, throne visions, and apocalypse – which correspond to well-known visionary moments in the Bible. To take one example, there is an echo of the vision of Ezekiel 1 in the letter to Butts: Ezekiel, in exile from his homeland, lying by the banks of the river Chebar, has a vision of God; here Blake, who has just left London – his physical and spiritual home of the previous forty years – is on the shores of the sea, also having a vision of God (the Ezekiel scene is an important topos elsewhere in Blake's work too). There is also common ground between Ezekiel's vision and that of the Solitary. The exiled Ezekiel experiences a 'Merkabah' vision, that is, a vision of the divine throne or chariot of God, and this is also the form of the Solitary's vision in the *Excursion*:

> Right in the midst, where interspace appeared
> Of open court, an object like a throne
> Under a shining canopy of state
> Stood fixed. (l. 120–124)

There is an additional context that highlights this trope: the Solitary's vision is an explicit counterpart to the New Jerusalem vision of Revelation (3:12, 21:2 ff). John describes the sudden appearance of the city, its glorious form, shining 'like unto a stone most precious, even like a jasper stone, clear as crystal' and so on (Rev 21:11).

These details are paralleled by Wordsworth's 'mighty city' whose fabric was 'it seemed of diamond and of gold, / With alabaster domes, and silver spires' (ll. 94, 98–9). Moreover, at the centre of John's vision in Revelation is the throne of God surrounded by the four beasts (Rev 4:2 ff), and again, this vision of the throne (itself modelled on the Merkabah vision of Ezekiel 1) is picked up by Wordsworth at the centre of the *Excursion* passage (see above).[16] So, the Solitary's vision has strong similarities to that of John of Patmos, and also explicitly points us to Isaiah and Ezekiel via the reference to the 'Hebrew prophets [. . .] in vision' (ll. 126–7).

I will return to the figure of Jesus shortly, but first wish to consider a second striking similarity between the Blake and Wordsworth poems and to the visions of Paul the apostle and John of Patmos. Both Paul and John were, according to their own accounts, caught up into heaven. John writes:

> After this I looked, and, behold, a door was opened in heaven: and the first voice which I heard was as it were of a trumpet talking with me; which said, Come up hither, and I will shew thee things which must be hereafter. And immediately I was in the spirit: and, behold, a throne was set in heaven, and one sat on the throne. (Rev 4:1–2)

And Paul writes:

> I knew a man in Christ above fourteen years ago, (whether in the body, I cannot tell; or whether out of the body, I cannot tell: God knoweth;) such an one caught up to the third heaven. [. . .] How that he was caught up into paradise, and heard unspeakable words, which it is not lawful for a man to utter. [. . .] Of such an one will I glory: yet of myself I will not glory, but in mine infirmities. (2Cor 12:2–5)

Both the Blake and Wordsworth poems are concerned with a transformed heaven and earth such as that found in Revelation, and what is disclosed to Wordsworth's Solitary is closely related to what is disclosed to Blake. In both the poem to Butts and in *The Excursion* passage, the protagonists have a vision looking down from a heavenly perspective onto human life below them, a perspective that strongly echoes the elevation of John of Patmos and Paul, each of whom is caught up into heaven.

To return to the figure of Jesus that Blake is absorbed into. This is perhaps the most complicated facet of Blake's vision, and its complexity may correlate to its historical specificity. Blake's vision is organized around the idea of seeing particles of light, which then manifest as 'men'; these men then combine as one man in the figure of Jesus, who then absorbs Blake. There are obvious biblical precedents for this correlation between Jesus and light, not only in, for example, John the evangelist's description of Jesus being 'the true Light, which lighteth every man that cometh into the world' (John 1:9), but also in Saul's blinding vision of light that is Jesus:

> And as he journeyed, he came near Damascus: and suddenly there shined round about him a light from heaven: And he fell to the earth, and heard a voice saying unto him, Saul, Saul, why persecutest thou me? And he said, Who art thou, Lord? And the Lord said, I am Jesus. (Acts 9:3–5)

Blake also has a consistent theological basis for such an anthropomorphic vision. As Thomas Altizer puts it,

> if Christian revelation has the form of a man, it can scarcely give witness to a non-human God. Rather we must follow Blake and come to see that a Christian vision which unveils God as a man must culminate in an apocalyptic vision of 'The Great Humanity Divine'.[17]

It is unsurprising then that Blake's vision is, as Damrosch puts it, an 'epiphany of Jesus'[18]. But what of the historical specificity I mentioned? Donald Ault has discussed in detail the critique of a Newtonian worldview that Blake is engaged in here, and the process of atoms becoming men, becoming divine, is a re-baptism of an agnostic cosmology: all things are reunited through a reclamation of the universe by Jesus. And it is a *human* form that the universe takes.[19]

To summarize the argument of this chapter: Blake and Wordsworth did not take drugs, and should not be described as 'mystics' in a casual way. Mystical experiences are diverse, not homogeneous. To think about the religious character of their writing it is more helpful to look at the range of biblical allusions in their texts, some of which I have touched on here. 'Religious experience' is, at a fundamental level, an encounter with – or within – a tradition. In the case of the present discussion, this is striking in the way that Blake and Wordsworth have internalized – among other parts of the Judaeo-Christian tradition – the writings of Ezekiel, Isaiah, Paul, and John of Patmos. This means that even if we can say little with certainty about the biographical or historical reality of these religious visions, we *can* talk with certainty about the textual religious worldview of which they are a part. Seen in this light, Blake and Wordsworth are no longer solitary prophets wandering the face of the earth, they are once again, as poets, 'men speaking to men' as Wordsworth has it; and they are also men *listening* to men, for it is through attending to the words and actions of their forbears that they themselves have heard the voice of God.

CHAPTER 7

RELIGION

Despite being a book about 'religion' none of the chapters so far has offered an empirically-grounded discussion of what 'religion' is – instead, each one has defined the matter according to its own lights. By contrast, this chapter draws on a range of sociological studies to present a thumbnail sketch of contemporary British and US religion, focussing on the terms 'religion' and 'spirituality' before going on to consider how those factors interoperate in the writings of Blake and Wordsworth. In brief, I will argue that a statistical majority of British people identify as having a theistic belief, but simultaneously maintain an outlook that is anti-organizational, anti-ecclesiastical, and rooted in private 'spiritual' experience. That correlates, I will suggest, to a contemporary disjunction between 'spirituality' and 'religion' evident in studies of the US scene. I will go on to suggest that these binaries are not a modern phenomenon, but are continuous with the religious outlook of Blake and Wordsworth, poets who are appealing not because they are unworldly mystics, but, by contrast, because their writings embody central characteristics of modern 'religious' life. I begin, however, with the question of what religion is in Britain, two centuries after these poems were written.[1]

In terms of breadth, if not depth, of coverage, the fullest contemporary survey of religious belief in Britain is the 2001 census. The census summary noted that there are '37.3 million people in England and Wales who state their religion as Christian.'[2] A large number, and one that does not immediately reveal the discrepancy between belief and practice presented in more detailed, long-term studies such as those summarized by Grace Davie, whereby belief in God in 1990 in Great Britain is 71 per cent, but frequency of church attendance (at least once a week for the same study) is 13 per cent,[3] meaning that only 18.3 per cent of people who believe in God go to church.[4] Writing on religion in post-War Britain, Davie muses that it is 'hard to discover a field of enquiry containing a greater number of apparent contradictions'. She continues:

> These contradictions show up most clearly in a series of questions. Why is it, for example, that the majority of British people – in common with many other Europeans – persist in believing (if only in an ordinary God), but see no need to participate with even minimal regularity in their religious institutions? Indeed most people in this country [Britain] – whatever their denominational allegiance – express their religious sentiments by staying away from, rather than going to, their places of worship. On the other hand, relatively few British people have opted out of religion altogether: out and out atheists are rare.[5]

Many individuals prefer to identify as 'spiritual' rather than 'religious', as the former permits a theistic outlook without commitment to the forms of life associated with the latter. Numerous sociological studies have examined this binary of religious belief and religious (non) practice, and it can be constructively related to studies made in the US that contrast or compare 'spirituality' with 'religion', for the reason that these terms seem to be differentiated in a way that has common elements with the British scene. How then is this religious / spiritual binary borne out by recent sociological studies of religion? B. J. Zinnbauer et al's 1997 study of this subject 'Religion and Spirituality: Unfuzzying the fuzzy' sought to measure 'how individuals define the terms *religiousness* and *spirituality*', and to examine these definitions in the light of the US sample's 'different demographic, religio / spiritual, and psychosocial variables'.[6] The sample comprised 346 individuals of different religious backgrounds, and found that spirituality and religiousness are diversely and conflictingly described[7], reflecting the range of meanings those terms have to individuals, such that to some, 'religiousness meant church attendance, to others it meant acts of altruism, and to others it meant performing certain rituals', while popular references to spirituality 'have included elements such as interest in angels, New Age interest in crystals and psychic readings, and evangelical or Pentecostal religious experiences'[8]. The authors go on:

> Whereas religiousness historically included both individual and institutional elements, spirituality is now commonly regarded as an individual phenomenon and identified with such things as personal transcendence, supraconscious sensitivity, and meaningfulness (Spilka and McIntosh 1996). Religiousness, in contrast, is now often described narrowly as formally structured and identified with religious institutions and prescribed theology and rituals.[9]

The Zinnbauer study finds – confirming its own hypothesis – that the terms 'religiousness' and 'spirituality' present related but different concepts, and what is particularly interesting to the present study is the cultural values that are associated with these distinctions:

> As predicted, religiousness was found to be associated with higher levels of authoritarianism, religious orthodoxy, intrinsic religiousness, parental religious attendance, self-righteousness, and church attendance. In line with predictions, spirituality was associated with a different

set of variables: mystical experiences, New Age beliefs and practices, higher income, and the experience of being hurt by clergy. (Zinnbauer et al., 561)

In short, religion is associated in such studies with characteristics that tend to be perceived as negative in popular culture (authoritarianism, self-righteousness, and so on), while spirituality tends to be associated with cultural positives: mystical experiences, individual liberty, self development, and so forth. In Britain, similarly, a majority of people hold a belief in God, but eschew the regulation and structured experience associated with institutional religious frameworks. But how has this situation come to pass? Inevitably, some sociologists have sought to find a historical explanation for this binary, arguing that it is a modern phenomenon, and – perhaps unsurprisingly given the discussion so far in this book – that sociological account has focussed specifically on the 1960s, a decade which is viewed, Marler and Hadaway argue, as 'the watermark of twentieth century religious revitalization and change: a "third Dis-establishment," a "third Great Awakening," or even the "second Reformation"'.[10] In addition, shifting socio-economic circumstances and sociocultural 'trends towards deinstitutionalization, individualization, and globalization have been used by a number of authors, including Parmagent (1999), to explain increased attention to "spirituality" and the diminished cultural presence of traditional religious institutions'. Moreover, they continue, 'sociologists of religion, notably Roof (1993), identify so-called baby boomers as the primary carriers of a late modern American religion that is self-reflexive, unabashedly consumerist, small-group based, and creatively syncretistic.'[11] This mystical-psychedelic-syncretistic configuration has, as we have seen in the preceding chapters, quarried Blake and Wordsworth (among numerous other writers) for its sacred texts.

But is this really a distinctly modern phenomenon? What is noticeable here is that this supposedly modern distinction between religious and spiritual sensibilities is already evident within Blake's and Wordsworth's writing. But not here alone: there are other, earlier analogues for this supposed shift, and Zinnbauer's claim that historically, 'spirituality was not distinguished from religiousness until the rise of secularism in [the twentieth] century, and a popular disillusionment with religious institution as a hindrance to personal experiences of the sacred'[12] may be less than clear cut. In Chapter 5, we have already seen an (albeit late) nineteenth-century example of J. Trevor feeling a tension between the religious and the mystical. Nancy Easterlin finds a still earlier instance in the early nineteenth-century writings of Friedrich Schleiermacher, whose works seek to establish 'the separation of inner religious experience from church ritual and authority, insisting on the pure ontological status of the former and the secondary and symbolic nature of the latter'. 'Hence', Easterlin writes, 'religion came to be defined as a core of feeling not necessarily attached to a body of beliefs and practices'.[13]

Easterlin argues that the split between (i) 'inner' religion / spirituality, and (ii) 'outer' religion / ritual worship originates in the Romantic period itself. She writes suggestively of this bifurcation:

> The entry of the word religion into common parlance in the nineteenth century itself signals the loss in Western culture of the perceived unity such a term logically suggests. The category of religion, from the romantic period forward, encompasses nothing like this formal certainty, for while it retains connotations of a higher unity, it no longer necessarily implies an integrated understanding of the personal, social, and supernatural dimensions of experience. Rather, we have inherited from the nineteenth century the habit

of using the term *religion* for one or the other of the aspects implied by a total metaphysic and spiritual commitment; our resultingly ambiguous and contradictory sense of the term coupled with our persistent use of it indicates the marked degree to which we share the metaphysical uneasiness of the last century and the hope for some unity that the word *religion* should logically reflect. Is religion best described in terms of individual experience, as a state of feeling or of heightened consciousness? Or as various social practices, established orthodoxies, belief systems affirmed and perpetuated through ritual practices? As we superficially conceive it, religion in some kind of working order must fulfil both of these functions, encompassing the personal, social, and supernatural dimensions of experience and reality; but it is in fact the paradoxical discrepancy between religion defined, on the one hand, as affective experience – states of heightened consciousness or intuition of the divine, for example – and, on the other, as organized belief systems that describes the characteristic and manifestly problematic religiousness of romanticism.[14]

What I want to take from Easterlin here is the fact that in these Romantic works, both aspects of this binary are evident and at play with one another. In fact, it is not simply a binary here, as there is a consciousness in the literature under discussion of the multiple facets of religious experience: individual, corporate, mystical, pragmatic, and that these 'supernatural dimensions' become manifest among the domestic arrangements of everyday life – a walk in the hills, making a sketch on the beach. In Blake's and Wordsworth's writings we see these different facets of religious life (which for the statistical majority now appear to be discrete entities) still in relationship with one another, even if that relationship may be (as Easterlin argues) one of doubt.

To recap: both the US and British studies identify a religious / spiritual or religion / belief distinction. This distinction is also evident in the Blake and Wordsworth poems: each containing a protagonist who experiences a mystical vision in a setting that is natural rather than ecclesiastical. So, both manifest the characteristically modern sensibility of believing in God / spiritual experience, but being alienated from institutional religious settings. In this respect, they anticipate the puzzling discrepancy between belief and practice outlined by Grace Davie at the beginning of this chapter. However, they also do something more than this. At the point in time that Blake and Wordsworth are writing, although the religious / spiritual binary is already visible in outline, it has not yet fragmented into the modern situation depicted by Easterlin, whereby 'religion' is a word that struggles – and fails – to incorporate 'the personal, social, and supernatural dimensions of experience'. Wordsworth and Blake may not achieve such an integration, but the sense that all the different parts of life – the intellectual, sensual, political, domestic, geographical, interpersonal, social, and so on – are interrelated in some greater spiritual way, is fundamental to their works. One of the striking characteristics of Blake's illuminated books, in particular, is the way in which his great religious epics bring together every aspect of his experience: in the words quoted earlier from the end of the poem to Butts, 'all I ever had known before me bright shone'. As I will suggest a little later, this is one of the special values to a modern readership of the two poets' writings: that they express a vision which contains, among other things, all the doubt of modern religious belief, but one which does not reduce religion to the media caricature discussed in the introduction to this book.

But to come to the poems themselves, how has this narrowed understanding of religion played out in the interpretation of these specific works? I would like to suggest that in many instances this disarticulated modern understanding of religion has led to monochrome 'religious' readings of these poems, whereby the writing is considered to be, for example, either mystical *or* theological *or* political. This has been evident even within the course of this book, as the chapters so far have bifurcated along a spiritual / religious divide. In the case of the earlier chapter focussing on mystical experience, there was little interest in the social, formal, corporate, institutional facets of religious life, while the 'theological' discussion in the last chapter required obviating the mystical dimensions of these poems. In other words, if we approach these poems with a syncretistic / mystical paradigm in mind, then that is likely to produce a particular type of reading. Likewise, if we approach with a more orthodox paradigm (say, that of Anglicanism), then we will get another. Neither of these is wrong. It is just that – to borrow Blake – each takes a portion of existence and fancies that the whole. The limitation is that these characteristically modern disarticulated religious models are read into, then back out of the poems themselves.[15] As a result, the history of interpretation of the religious character of both the Blake and Wordsworth poems is characterized – with a few notable exceptions which I will draw on presently – by a lack of attention to tone and context. As the earlier discussion suggested, in many cases the poems have been read as reports of encounters with a spiritual plane, and the sense of their ambiguity, irony, and in the case of Blake, their humour, has been overlooked. Attending to the tone, however, diversifies and humanizes the poems, moving them beyond monotone syncretistic or orthodox stereotypes, and restoring the complex, multifaceted, questioning engagement with religion that they actually present.

What then do we know about the tone of these poems? In the case of 'To my friend Butts' we are dealing with a quite widely-anthologized poem, but one that is usually abridged, and rarely set forth in the context of the original letter. In fact, the letter is a reply to what De Selincourt called 'a cordial, jocular epistle in not too perfect taste'[16] in which Butts contemplates Mrs Blake being 'embraced by Neptune'. So, we know the audience for the poem (Butts); the location (Felpham); and the date, and all this is helpful in reading the tone which is friendly, warm, and playful, with Blake describing himself as 'the determined advocate of religion and humility'. Blake is gently mocking a conventional religious stance here, and within that mode he gives his extraordinary vision of God. This playful tone is easily lost sight of: if we were to subscribe to the religious / spiritual binary above, it would be tempting (as many readers have done) to make Blake the great enemy of 'institutional religion' and the great advocate of individual spiritual liberty. But matters are more complex than that.

Blake clearly did regard the church as highly problematic because of the way religion has been used to obstruct social justice, but this will not conveniently map onto an internal-spiritual / external-religious dyad because as so many of Blake's poems make clear, the internal and external are part of the same continuum.[17] Therefore the division, the binary of public / private or individual / corporate does not quite make sense in his terms. This is evident on a textual level as the last chapter suggested: the experience he recounts seems highly individual, but the language through which it is recounted is 'religious' or corporate – it is the imagery of the Bible. So there is in Blake an antagonism towards enslaving or tyrannical systems (such as the church), but this is not part of a binary predicated on a sort of 'free' spiritual experience represented by vision. Rather, this religious experience is a constellation of all sorts of factors and feelings shining at different magnitudes. For example, despite its cosmic elements, Blake's vision remains domestic, and in this respect is radically different from, say, the apocalyptic vision of John of Patmos. What Blake sees from earth is heaven, but when he is caught up into heaven what he sees is his village, his cottage, and the 'shadows' of his wife and friends: the eternal forms of these domestic relations, of everything he has ever seen. As a rehabilitation of the earth, of humanity, of Blake himself, of our relation with God, it remains light, friendly, amicable and has the gentleness of Traherne. That closing image of Blake seeing *everything* is like one of his snapshots of eternity such as his paintings of 'A Vision of the Last Judgment' (1808) and 'The Sea of Time and Space' (1821), but it has the gentleness of 'Jacob's Ladder' (c. 1805).

The Wordsworth poem is similarly complex. It has been abridged and anthologized throughout its history (as has been done in this book) as if it stands on its own, and we can take it to be a first-person account of a vision in which the author is the narrator. Alison Hickey puts it this way:

This passage is often singled out as a moment of visionary grandeur uncharacteristic of this poem. Its appearance in De Quincey's *Confessions of an English Opium Eater* is no doubt partly responsible for its being read as a set piece, often with little or no consideration for its implications of its being communicated by the Solitary, as opposed to Wordsworth himself or another character.[18]

So, although for almost two centuries the extract has served readers as an example of Wordsworth's poetic power and mystical vision, this paradigm is not borne out by the text itself, as what this usage of the text misses is that the vision is symbolically linked in the larger poem to other aspects of the Solitary's life. For example, close to the Solitary's dwelling place there is a sequestered nook that contains, among other things, a rural seat with a sort of canopy over it. This has been built by the Solitary himself. The significance of this is that the divine throne vision discussed at the end of the last chapter is clearly a sort of magnified beatified version of the Solitary's own garden seat, of his own domestic arrangements.[19] While this does not negate the 'value' of the vision (it may, in fact, enhance it, as it is a religious vision that can incorporate doubt and uncertainty), it does change our perspective on it. There is a new kind of ambiguity about the epiphany, which may be central to the character of the religious vision itself, but which we can only discover via the Solitary's life, *not* via Wordsworth's life. But this too complicates matters, for within the domestic setting of *The Excursion*, the speaker is not the self-authenticating poet, not any sort of spiritual guide or guru, but the anti-hero of the piece, and is depicted as a scornful apostate. At the time of the vision he is not full of the milk of human kindness, rather he is seething with anger about the potentially fatal petty machinations of a local house-wife, and the vision does not, despite its provenance, have the effect of an apocalyptic transformation of his sensibilities. As J. R. Watson argues, the Solitary appears unable to *feel* the vision:

> The vision, and its description, suggests a capacity to see but not to feel. The Solitary can see a spectacle like that of Ezekiel or Isaiah, and he even sees the vale as transformed from a habitation of man into a place of blessed spirits; but in spite of this he is not prophetic – the sight is 'such *as* by Hebrew Prophets were beheld' – and he draws back from prophecy into self-questioning.[20]

As if this were not enough , the text openly brings out its own deep ambiguity later in Book III of *The Excursion* when the Solitary is describing his experience of the French Revolution. He says:

From that abstraction I was rouzed, – and how?   715
Even as a thoughtful Shepherd by a flash
Of lightening startled in a gloomy cave
Of these wild hills. For, lo! the dread Bastile,
With all the chambers in its horrid Towers,
Fell to the ground: – by violence o'erthrown   720
Of indignation; and with shouts that drowned
The crash it made in falling! From the wreck
A golden Palace rose, or seemed to rise,
The appointed Seat of equitable Law
And mild paternal Sway. The potent shock   725
I felt: the transformation I perceived,
As marvellously seized as in that moment
When, from the blind mist issuing, I beheld
Glory – beyond all glory ever seen,
Confusion infinite of heaven and earth,   730
Dazzling the soul! Meanwhile, prophetic harps
In every grove were ringing, 'War shall cease;
'Did ye not hear that conquest is abjured? [']²¹

In describing his response to the French Revolution, the Solitary's imagery likens the latter again to the New Jerusalem (the golden palace) in the same sort of language as the vision of the storm ('confusion infinite of heaven and earth'), and even repeats verbatim the line 'Glory – beyond all glory ever seen' which now becomes the marker of a false apocalypse. We also have 'prophetic harps', the Solitary is 'from the blind mist issuing', and at the centre of the vision, yet another throne, this time the 'appointed seat of equitable law / And mild paternal sway'. There is an excellent discussion of these complexities in Alison Hickey's *Impure Conceits*²² in which the author not only shows the parallels in imagery and language between the Solitary's own vision and the petty details of his everyday life, but also demonstrates the poem's dramatic power and cunning in enabling us to forget that parallel as readers:

> As readers we enact this doubleness by forgetting the Solitary as we experience his vision: it is difficult to maintain a real sense of the continuity between the sceptical character who lives in an apartment cluttered with 'implements of ordinary use' and builds baby-houses and the character who loses himself in this vision. But that is precisely the point: the Solitary's occasional loss of self – his 'self-withdrawal,' his death as a character – makes up one side of his function as a rhetorical principle. The Solitary is the figure of irreducible dualisms, of 'either-or'.[23]

The poetic vision is, in short, tonally complex, and it provides a religious experience that incorporates both epiphany and irony, doubt and faith, and it happens to a once-happy Christian who is now alienated from both society and the church. The divine vision of the poem may be exactly the sort of sensory experience that many modern individuals would reckon authentic, and would crave for or seek out, but (and brilliantly) it is the vision of an individual who has an entirely modern sceptical disposition. It is, finally, a vision that – unlike the myriad human forms of Blake's vision and the crowded scenes of Revelation – is devoid of human life: the Solitary's isolation is extended into a deserted divine epiphany reflecting his own chosen isolation.

What can be said then about the religious experiences narrated by these poems? At first it might seem that the presence of doubt, humour, irony, and so forth must undermine or invalidate the significance of these visions. But that is only the case if we have a narrow (and characteristically modern) sense of what constitutes religion. What these poems can show us, if we let them, is a model of religion that exists with and through all elements of human life. Its existence does not require a stable, sombre tone (though it might include this), nor does it require a specific location (it is open to place), nor does it necessitate vanquishing basic human experiences such as doubt and ambiguity.

One result of the generosity and breadth of the religious character of these poems is that they are easily appropriated by those wishing to exemplify mystical experience, those wishing to show the orthodoxy and biblicism of the two writers, and those wishing to find validating precedents for the individualistic epiphany of the psychedelic trip. However, the real value of these poems is, I would suggest, the liberating knowledge that they can be all of these things simultaneously, and no one of those aspects negates the others. Moreover, it is in this respect that the poems are of particular value to a present-day largely theistic population immersed in a culture that continuously attempts to reduce religion to a caricatured binary, in response to which individuals are cajoled into taking sides. Blake and Wordsworth offer an open-handed way out of this dead end, not because they are (solely) seers or mystics, but because they (also) anticipate religious positions – individualistic, anti-institutional, anti-ecclesiastical, with a grounding in personal spirituality, that puts them at the median of twenty-first century British religious experience. The tonal ambiguity and internal conflict of Blake's and Wordsworth's poetry offers a space in which the living legacy of a set of post-Enlightenment conflicts over religion can be constructively played out.

CHAPTER 8

IN CONCLUSION

Much of the recent scholarship on Romantic religion has worked with the material history of that subject. The extensive work on Blake's relationship to the Swedenborg church and Moravianism offers one example; Wordsworth's later relationship to various figures within the churches, another.[1] This historical work provides a context for better understanding the discursive situation of the poets' works, and vice versa. There's an analogue in a different line of scholarly enquiry that has sought to delineate the religion of these poets as theology, that is, as organized bodies of ideas.[2]

Rather than translating Blake's and Wordsworth's poetic argument with religion into either a period discourse, or a coherent structure of belief, my aim in this book has been to open a different route into the topic. My own view is that the 'religion' of Blake's and Wordsworth' writings is not (primarily) about the assertion of propositions, nor is it (primarily) a record of religious belief; rather it is the linguistic enactment of a religious sensibility. To clarify this statement, I need to say a little more about what I mean by 'religion' in this context.

One way I have addressed the question of religion in this book is by enacting different types of readerly / critical responses to the religious character of Blake's and Wordsworth's poetry. I have done this in an attempt to grapple with the fact that the subject of religion is approached quite differently according to the disciplinary context: theologians, biographers, sociologists, historians and so on tend to address different aspects of the same materials, using different approaches, and drawing different conclusions.[3] Rather than looking for a master discipline which can unify these discourses, my aim has been to emphasize that these approaches do not simply differ in terms of their conclusions, but that in their very outworking they produce qualitatively distinct experiential worlds for their users: reading about a poet's religion in a biography is fundamentally different from feeling one has personally attained a comparable experience through the use of psychedelics, and both are fundamentally different from the experience of reinterpreting the poetry by relating it in detail to an inherited biblical or theological tradition. These interpretive experiences cannot be adequately expressed in one another's terms, and to dismiss one in order to validate another narrows, rather than broadens understanding. In other words, in the attempt to understand better what religion is, each of these approaches offers something *experientially* important that needs to be felt in its own right. Openness to these different experiential facets is, I am suggesting, central to what Wordsworth and Blake offer us, and it is a gift that helps us to see the character of religious experience in three dimensions (regardless of whether or not we consider ourselves to be 'religious'), rather than the two dimensions of those public debates in which antagonists seek to demolish each other's world views. For this reason, I think attentiveness to these experiential particularities is more useful than thinking about, say, a unifying category such as 'aesthetic pleasure', when the latter term – like 'religion' itself – is required to carry so much that it can achieve very little.

This tolerance and inclusiveness that I have been discussing is evident from the outset in both poets' writings. *Lyrical Ballads* and *Songs of Innocence and of Experience* are not about simply providing 'aesthetic pleasure' (whatever that term might mean), but offer instead an emotionally remarkably diverse set of engagements with children, the outcast, the mentally ill, the enslaved, the city, the country, warfare, and peace: they are inclusive and open-hearted. These characteristics are even more strongly evident in the two poets' later works. Blake's *Jerusalem*, to take one example, is explicitly, outspokenly, a religious text, yet it is anything but cloistered: everything is included, from Blake's home, to whales, to beetles, to the Congo – the lot. Wordsworth in his very different way, wishes to be similarly inclusive in his great work which he specifically likens to a Gothic church and its 'little Cells, Oratories, and sepulchral Recesses'.[4]

Twentieth-century philosophy provides another means to think about this topic, particularly the work of Ludwig Wittgenstein (1889–1951) and Richard Rorty (1931–2007). Both philosophers (along with many others) separately propounded anti-essentialist views of language that regard it as a human creation. The crux of this argument is that there is an asymmetry between world and language. Take 'the world' to signify the phenomenal universe, the totality of what is 'out there' that exists independently of the human mind. Language is a series of attempts to represent that world. However, language is a human phenomenon and does not exist in a fixed relationship to the world, but is rather a series of evolving linguistic approximations of the world, and one that functions in quite different ways in different areas of life. To put it another way, the phenomenal universe exists independently of human thoughts and emotions,[5] and does *not* have a natural language of its own: we provide our own languages in our encounter with it. There is no fixed relationship between the two.

Wittgenstein and Rorty draw attention to the error of assuming that language operates in the same manner in all its different areas of usage. A simple example of this would be to imagine that all words are ostensive definitions: that they all point to objects. This might work for some words (like 'sea' or 'table'), but is full of difficulties, as Wittgenstein demonstrates at length in *Philosophical Investigations* when it comes to others (how might we point to words such as 'future', 'ouch', or 'nuance'?) Different kinds of human activity, including different types of academic discipline, require different vocabularies, and these vocabularies are what Wittgenstein describes (non-dismissively, despite the lightness of the term) as 'language games'. In the same way that chess, tennis, and solitaire bear similarities but have distinct internal laws and logics, different disciplinary discourses (what Rorty calls 'vocabularies' and Wittgenstein calls 'language games') have different rules and different functions. The 'vocabulary' of, say, quantum computing necessarily differs from that of, say systematic theology; they are incommensurable: one cannot be adequately communicated in the vocabulary of the other.

What is important here is the recognition that the languages we develop in our engagement with the world are contingent and provisional, even in the cases of the natural sciences and theology, in which new vocabularies continue to extend, or modify, or supersede the old as our experience of the world itself extends, reduces, or changes. The frustration – for those who would like a stable, fixed relationship between word and world – is that we cannot get outside language in order to decide how vocabularies correlate to each other, and there is no meta-language that can stand over and above them, or into which they will ultimately be resolved.[6] As with the problems about history raised in Chapter 3, this is not a despairing relativism, nor a disavowal of the value or necessity of language. Rather it is an acknowledgment that the world cannot speak or decide between different language games on our behalf. As Rorty puts it, 'The world does not speak. Only we do'.[7]

The relevance of this philosophical material to the wider discussion of this book can be made clearer with

religious one, but rather than take a religious paradigm from a sociologist, anthropologist, or historian, I will take one from the poets themselves. The paradigm I wish to conclude with, is the idea that 'religion' is essentially concerned with the relationship between the individual and God, or, to put it another way, between the part and the whole. My suggestion is not capricious, it is at the centre of Blake's work. He describes the 'divine vision' in *Jerusalem*, for example, as follows:

Mutual in one anothers love and wrath all renewing
We live as One Man; for contracting our infinite senses
We behold multitude; or expanding: we behold as one,
As One Man all the Universal Family; and that One Man
We call Jesus the Christ: and he in us, and we in him,
Live in perfect harmony in Eden the land of life,
Giving, recieving, and forgiving each others trespasses.[12]

That model of simultaneous unity and particularity is familiar from many religious texts, including, for example, Paul's model of the Body of Christ.[13] Working against that reconciliation are those things which fracture that dynamic unity: war, sin, hatred, enmity, the treatment of others (humans and all forms of life) as objects for consumption, pollution, belligerence, ethnic cleansing, and the catalogues of violence presented to us by the media day by day. And in contrast to these are those things – however trite it sounds – that reconnect the parts to each other and to the whole: the mystical sense, peacemaking, forgiveness, reconciliation, understanding, love.

The emphasis in this relationship between parts within the whole is not on uniformity, but on fraternal coexistence: the members of Paul's body of Christ (1 Corinthians 12) retain their distinctiveness, and this idea is central to Blake's myth. We have seen a version of it in the poem to Butts in which the anthropomorphized beams of light coalesce to form the body of Christ. But this is by no means exclusively a Christian insight – as renowned Buddhist teacher Jack Kornfield writes, 'We must see that spirituality is a continual movement away from compartmentalization and separation and toward embracing all of life.'[14]

I am not suggesting that this paradigm governs the totality of either poet's work, or that it is present everywhere in that work, but rather that it is a key question of their writings. Consider their great poems *Jerusalem* and *The Excursion*. *The Excursion* takes as a central theme the question of the part and the whole that I have been discussing. The quandary is embodied by the Solitary: it is evident in his very name. He is a part broken off from the whole, an individual once part of a religious community (a pastor), of a family (father, husband, son), of a society and nation (the army), and so on. Now through disaster and disillusionment, bereavement and failure, he is broken off from all of these: he is a geographically isolated atheist. He is the Solitary. The poem asks, how can he be restored to the universe in which he dwells? *The Excursion* offers no easy solutions, but is a meditation on these religious questions. *Jerusalem*, like many of Blake's works, mythologizes a similar process: Albion, an earthly counterpart of Jesus falls into a sleep, and is broken up through a process of violent splitting into a series of components – shadows and emanations – each of which believes he or she can dwell separately, isolated from one another. Blake, like Wordsworth, conceives this set of divisions as a religious matter, and reflects on how it occurs, and how it may be redeemed. The power of this poetry lies in its dialectical and polyvocal character: it enacts the interplay of different aspects of life, making a seamless garment, but allowing their differences – however painful – to show through. Deanne Westbrook helpfully writes:

> Poetic language has no option but to attempt to express not thought, not feeling, not image (concrete object), but the significance of the compound experience, [as De Quincey names it], the involute, in which the parts are "incapable of being disentangled".[15]

It is this model that I have emulated in this book, by attempting to create a dialogue between a range of positions on the topic of Blake's and Wordsworth's religion, while maintaining the distinctness and disagreements of their positions. I have also tried to show how a multiplicity of tones and genres coexist, struggle, and cooperate within the poems themselves. Finally, I have suggested that this relationship between the individual and the total, between particularity and unity, and between the parts that make up the whole is of the essence of religion itself.

What literature can achieve – as these poets show – is to take us closer to a depiction of a multifaceted human universe than any single discipline can.[16] Such a depiction can be neither simply realist nor historical, for although these are both ways to approach that human truth, that truth will always exceed them. It is the open-minded generosity of spirit that makes this poetry of such value here: by giving us a space in which fiction and fact, reason and energy, history and fantasy, faith and doubt are in dialogue rather than in dispute with one another, Blake and Wordsworth enable us to encounter religion as a place in which to find again ourselves and our communities, our fallenness and our redemption, our damaged human solitariness and our restoration to one another in the human form of God.

ACKNOWLEDGEMENTS

Thanks to those who discussed ideas, or kindly read and gave helpful feedback on drafts of the book: Carolyn Burdett, Jessica Fay, Hong Hui Ying, Elisabeth Jessen, Mark Knight, Emma Mason, and (for many years of conversation about Blake and hermeneutics) Chris Rowland; for the warm memories of Lancaster in the early 90s: Mao Ang, Killer Robinson, Eric Szmyt; and for their great friendship during the latter stages of this book: Ang Bah Bee, Ang Cheng Eng, Matthew Chambers, David and Helen Cooper, Tom Pellizzari, Bertram P., Birgit Scheidle, Christine Smyth, Dave Riley, Carol, Keith, and Fergus Roberts, Shirley Tan, Nick and Sheenagh Thorpe, Catherine Rowland, P. C. Sue and Dave Wollen. Thanks to Gavin Band for his time and mathematical genius. Finally, special thanks to my sister, Hooi Hooi.

NOTES

CHAPTER 1

1 By 'hermeneutical' I mean here the interpretive paradigms that structure debates rather than the contents of the debates themselves.

2 I am *not* following James R. Kincaid's example in *Annoying the Victorians* (New York: Routledge, 1995) who begins his book: 'The essays that follow try very hard not to be law-abiding. To annoy: that is the aim' (p. 4). Kincaid's attack on critical paradigms is presented as an end in itself. His methods include 'juggling the question, refusing the answer, shuffling my own position, nudging you, pretending not to hear, making rude noises, asking dumb questions, trailing off, forgetting where we were, failing to attend, becoming bored, changing the rules to suit me, being inconsistent, courting incoherence' (p. 7).

3 A scholarly edition was published in 2008: *Excursion*.

CHAPTER 2

1 T. P. Hudson, A. P. Baggs and H. M. Warne, 'British History Online: Felpham' (2003) <http://www.british-history.ac.uk/report.aspx?compid=22943> [accessed 16 July 2008].

2 For the Scolfield incident see *BR* pp. 158ff.

3 WB to John Flaxman, 21 Sept 1800 (*E* p. 710).

4 WB to Thomas Butts, 23 Sept 1800 (*E* p. 711).

5 WB to Thomas Butts, 2 Oct 1800 (*E* pp. 711–13).

6 *The Excursion*, Book II, lines 764–916 in *Excursion*, pp. 99–103.

CHAPTER 3

1 See, for example, Jean H. Hagstrum, ' "The Wrath of the Lamb": A Study of William Blake's Conversions', in *From Sensibility to Romanticism*, ed. Harold Bloom and Frederick Whiley Hilles (New York: Oxford University Press, 1965), pp. 311–30; and Leopold Damrosch, *Symbol and Truth in Blake's Myth* (Princeton: Princeton University Press, 1980), pp. 46–9.

2 See Paul de Man, "Autobiography as De-facement," *Comparative Literature* 94, no. 5 (December 1979), pp. 919–30.

3 See Wordsworth's notes to Isabella Fenwick, in *Excursion*, p. 1218.
4 The issues I am referring to here are raised by (among others) Keith Jenkins, Hayden White and Richard Rorty.
5 Keith Jenkins, *On 'What Is History?': From Carr and Elton to Rorty and White* (London: Routledge, 1995), pp. 100, 134.
6 Except in so far as the poem refers to its own genesis and composition.
7 *The Times*, Wednesday, 1 Oct 1800, p. 3.
8 Historical tidal, lunar, and solar information derived from *Admiralty EasyTide* <http://easytide.ukho.gov.uk> [accessed 22 July 2008].
9 WB to Thomas Butts, 23 Sept 1800.
10 'To Butts', 4–5; 13.
11 *BR* p. 390, though this description given by Gilchrist in 1863.
12 *BR* p. 389.
13 WB to John Flaxman, 21 Sept 1800.
14 WB to George Cumberland, 1 Sept 1800.
15 'To Butts', 13.
16 'To Butts', 3, 7.
17 Alan Liu has written on this intractable problem of selecting and ordering historical evidence. See, for example, *The Laws of Cool* (Chicago: Chicago University Press, 2004).
18 See *Tate Online* < http://www.tate.org.uk/servlet/ViewWork? workid=1075> [accessed 20 July 2008].
19 Raymond Lister, *The Paintings of William Blake* (Cambridge: Cambridge University Press, 1986), p. 25.
20 I am making the assumption here that he wrote the poem on the day of the vision.

CHAPTER 4

Chapter Four uses a number of sources which are detailed towards the end of Chapter 5, but which I also give here. The lines beginning 'I had the Blake book on my lap' are adapted from Ginsberg, 'Experience' p. 122; the paragraph beginning 'The sensations from the mescaline' is adapted from Huxley's *Heaven and Hell* (in *Doors*, p. 60), and Ginsberg's 'Experience', p. 123. The quotation that constitutes the following paragraph is from Thomas Traherne's *Centuries of Meditations*, p. 152. The paragraph beginning 'All this, the feelings of connectedness' largely consists of quotes from Christopher

Mayhew MP, being filmed under the influence of mescaline and describing its effects on camera for a BBC documentary entitled *Panorama*. The paragraph beginning 'Seventeen years on' borrows in the loosest way from a range of passages in De Quincey's *Confessions*, *Suspiria*, and *English Mail-Coach*, while the final paragraph 'Ever since that experience' is taken almost verbatim from the final paragraph of G. Ray Jordan's 'LSD and Mystical Experiences' G. Ray Jordan published in the Oxford University Press, *Journal of Bible and Religion* (1963).

CHAPTER 5

1 William James, *Varieties of Religious Experience: A Study in Human Nature* (London: Routledge, 2002), p. 329; Stace in R. C. Zaehner, *Drugs, Mysticism and Make-Believe* (London: Collins, 1972), pp. 89–93.

2 James, *Varieties,* p. 39.

3 Quoted in James, *Varieties*, p. 343.

4 James, *Varieties,* p. 339.

5 James, *Varieties,* p. 340.

6 Caroline Frances Eleanor Spurgeon, *Mysticism in English Literature* (Cambridge: Cambridge University Press, 1913), p. 11.

7 F. C. Happold, *Mysticism: A Study and an Anthology*, rev. edn (London: Penguin, 1970), pp. 43, 91.

8 William Wordsworth, *The Pedlar. Tintern Abbey. The Two-Part Prelude*, ed. Jonathan Wordsworth (Cambridge: Cambridge University Press, 1985), p. 34*n*.

9 William A Ulmer, *The Christian Wordsworth, 1798–1805* (Albany, NY: State University of New York Press, 2001), p. 37.

10 J. Robert Barth, *Romanticism and Transcendence: Wordsworth, Coleridge, and the Religious Imagination* (Columbia, MO: University of Missouri Press, 2003), p. 64.

11 Henry Crabb Robinson, *Diary, Reminiscences, and Correspondence*, ed. Thomas Sadler, vol. 1, 3 vols., 2nd edn (London: Macmillan & Co., 1869), p. 434.

12 S. Foster Damon, *William Blake. His Philosophy and Symbols* (London: Constable & Co., 1924), p. 301.

13 Hazard Adams, *William Blake. A Reading of the Shorter Poems* (Seattle: University of Washington Press, 1963), p. 169.

14 Thomas J. J. Altizer, *The New Apocalypse: The Radical Christian Vision of William Blake* (East Lansing: Michigan State University Press, 1967), pp. 12ff.

15 Altizer, *Apocalypse*, p. 17.

16 David Wells, *A Study of William Blake's Letters* (Tübingen: Stauffenburg-Verlag, 1987), p. 75.

17 Damrosch, *Symbol,* p. 46.

18 Damrosch, *Symbol,* p. 47.

19 Damrosch, *Symbol,* pp. 47–9.

20 Damrosch, *Symbol,* p. 49.

21 For this reason, some writers prefer to call such drugs 'entheogens' meaning 'God containing'. See Huston Smith, *Cleansing the Doors of Perception: The Religious Significance of Entheogenic Plants and Chemicals* (New York: Jeremy P. Tarcher/Putnam, 2000), pp. xvi–xvii.

22 See Huston Smith's discussion of the infamous 'Good Friday' experiment (administering psilocybin and placebos to thirty theology professors and students in the context of the traditional Good Friday service at Boston University), and, less dramatically, of simply presenting readers with anonymous accounts of 'drug' and 'religious' experiences and asking them to decide which are which (Smith, *Cleansing*, pp. 99–105; pp. 21–2).

23 Thomas De Quincey, *The Works of Thomas De Quincey [Confessions of an English Opium-Eater]*, ed. Grevel Lindop, vol. 2, The Pickering masters (London: Pickering & Chatto, 2000), p. 43.

24 Marcus Boon, *The Road of Excess: A History of Writers on Drugs* (Cambridge, MA: Harvard University Press, 2002), p. 13.

25 See Alethea Hayter, *Opium and the Romantic Imagination* (London: Faber, 1968), and Martin Booth, *Opium: A History* (London: Simon & Schuster, 1996) for more detailed discussion of these cases.

26 Boon, *Writers*, pp. 91–2.

27 Hayter, *Opium*, p. 97.

28 Boon, *Excess*, pp. 232, 235, 237.

29 Boon, *Excess*, p. 250.

30 Boon, *Excess*, p. 250.

31 Smith, *Cleansing,* pp. 6–7.

32 Boon, *Excess*, p. 261.

33 Boon, *Excess*, p. 261.

paranoia, as they sometimes call it, we may have a *diabolical mysticism*, a sort of religious mysticism turned upside down. The same sense of ineffable importance in the smallest events, the same texts and words coming with new meanings, the same voices and visions and leadings and missions, the same controlling by extraneous powers; only this time the emotion is pessimistic: instead of consolations we have desolations; the meanings are dreadful; and the powers are enemies to life. It is evident that from the point of view of their psychological mechanism, the classic mysticism and these lower mysticisms spring from the same mental level, from that great subliminal or transmarginal region of which science is beginning to admit the existence, but of which so little is really known. That region contains every kind of matter: "seraph and snake" abide there side by side. To come from thence is no infallible credential. What comes must be sifted and tested, and run the gauntlet of confrontation with the total context of experience, just like what comes from the outer world of sense. Its value must be ascertained by empirical methods, so long as we are not mystics ourselves.' (James, *Varieties*, pp. 368–9).

14 Zaehner, *Mysticism*, p. 35.
15 Isaiah 11: 4–6, 9.
16 Isaiah 11 is also a prototype of the new heaven and new earth of Revelation 21.
17 Altizer, *Apocalypse*, p. 187.
18 Damrosch, *Symbol*, p. 46.
19 See Donald D. Ault, *Visionary Physics: Blake's Response to Newton* (Chicago: University of Chicago Press, 1974).

CHAPTER 7

1 NB though using the broad term 'religion' in this chapter, I am principally referring to Christianity, and I do not mean to suggest that this is the representative or exclusive belief system for the cultures under discussion.
2 Census information derived from *Census 2001– Ethnicity and religion in England and Wales* <http://www.statistics.gov.uk/census2001/profiles/commentaries/ethnicity.asp> [accessed 3 August 2008].
3 Grace Davie, 'Patterns of religion in Western Europe: an exceptional case', in *The Blackwell Companion to Sociology*

of Religion, ed. Richard K. Fenn, (Oxford: Blackwell, 2003), pp. 264–277 (pp. 267–8).

4 This is making the considerable assumption that all those who attend church believe in God.

5 Grace Davie, *Religion in Britain Since 1945: Believing Without Belonging* (Oxford: Blackwell, 1994), p. 2.

6 Brian J. Zinnbauer et al., 'Religion and Spirituality: Unfuzzying the Fuzzy', *Journal for the Scientific Study of Religion* 36, no. 4 (December, 1997), pp. 549–64 (p. 549).

7 Zinnbauer, 'Religion', p. 550.

8 Zinnbauer, 'Religion', p. 550.

9 Zinnbauer, 'Religion', p. 551.

10 Penny Long Marler and C. Kirk Hadaway, ' "Being Religious" or "Being Spiritual" in America: A Zero-Sum Proposition?', *Journal for the Scientific Study of Religion* 41, no. 2 (June 2002), pp. 289–300 (p. 289).

11 Marler and Hadaway, 'Being Religious', p. 289.

12 Zinnbauer, 'Religion', p. 550.

13 Nancy Easterlin, *Wordsworth and the Question of 'Romantic Religion'* (Lewisburg: Bucknell University Press, 1996), pp. 34–5; William James approaches religion from within the affective tradition established by Schleiermacher, and for this reason he tends to analyze states of mind irrespective of the institutional practices of his subjects.

14 Easterlin, *Wordsworth*, p. 29.

15 In Easterlin's view, such religious statements may actually be expressions of doubt: 'The romantic lyric to which I will soon turn is religious, then, in this particularly modern sense: it dramatically asserts authentic religious experience while simultaneously raising doubts about the genesis, ontological status, and social value of the experience' (Easterlin, *Wordsworth*, pp. 36–7).

16 Basil De Selincourt, *William Blake* (London: Duckworth, 1909), p. 274.

17 See, for example, the psychology of 'The Sick Rose' (*E* p. 22) and the *Innocence* 'Chimney Sweeper' (*E* p. 9).

18 Alison Hickey, *Impure Conceits: Rhetoric and Ideology in Wordsworth's 'Excursion'* (Stanford, CA: Stanford University Press, 1997), p. 64.

19 See the intriguing discussion of this in Hickey, *Impure*, pp. 264–8.

BIBLIOGRAPHY

Adams, Hazard, *William Blake. A Reading of the Shorter Poems* (Seattle: University of Washington Press, 1963).

Altizer, Thomas J. J., *The New Apocalypse: The Radical Christian Vision of William Blake* (East Lansing: Michigan State University Press, 1967).

Ault, Donald D., *Visionary Physics: Blake's Response to Newton* (Chicago: University of Chicago Press, 1974).

Ba Han, Maung, *William Blake, His Mysticism* (Philadelphia: R. West, 1917).

Barth, J. Robert, *Romanticism and Transcendence: Wordsworth, Coleridge and the Religious Imagination* (Columbia: University of Missouri Press, 2003).

Bentley, Gerald Eades, *The Stranger from Paradise: A Biography of William Blake* (New Haven: Yale University Press, 2001).

—, *Blake Records: Documents (1714–1841) Concerning the Life of William Blake (1757–1827) and His Family, Incorporating Blake Records (1969), Blake Records Supplement (1988), and Extensive Discoveries Since 1988,* 2nd edn (New Haven: Published for the Paul Mellon Centre for Studies in British Art by Yale University Press, 2004).

Blake, William, *The Complete Poetry and Prose of William Blake*, ed. David V. Erdman, Newly rev. edn (New York: Anchor Books, 1988).

Blakemore, Steven, 'De Quincey's Transubstantiation of Opium in the Confessions', *Massachusetts Studies in English* 9 (1984), pp. 32–41.

Boon, Marcus, *The Road of Excess: A History of Writers on Drugs* (Cambridge: Harvard University Press, 2002).

Booth, Martin, *Opium: A History* (London: Simon & Schuster, 1996).

Bruce, Harold, *William Blake in This World.* (London: Cape, 1925).

Bruce, Steve, *Religion in Modern Britain* (Oxford: Oxford University Press, 1995).

Chandler, James K., *England in 1819: The Politics of Literary Culture and the Case of Romantic Historicism* (Chicago: University of Chicago Press, 1998).

Clark, Elizabeth A., *History, Theory, Text: Historians and the Linguistic Turn* (Cambridge: Harvard University Press, 2004).

Crocket, Richard Wilfred, R. A. Sandison, and Alexander Walk, eds, *Hallucinogenic Drugs and Their Psychotherapeutic Use* (London: H. K. Lewis, 1963).

Damon, Samuel Foster, *William Blake. His Philosophy and Symbols* (London: Constable & Co., 1924).

Damrosch, Leopold Jr., *Symbol and Truth in Blake's Myth* (Princeton: Princeton University Press, 1980).

Davie, Grace, 'Patterns of Religion in Western Europe: An Exceptional Case', in *The Blackwell Companion to Sociology of Religion*, ed. Richard K. Fenn (Oxford: Blackwell, 2003).

—, *Religion in Britain Since 1945: Believing Without Belonging* (Oxford: Blackwell, 1994).

Davies, J. G., *The Theology of William Blake* (Oxford: Clarendon Press, 1948).

Davies, Keri, and Marsha Keith Schuchard, 'Recovering the Lost Moravian History of William Blake's Family', *Blake: An Illustrated Quarterly*, no. 38 (2004), pp. 36–42.

De Luca, Vincent, 'Satanic Fall and Hebraic Exodus: An Interpretation of De Quincey's "Revolt of the Tartars"', *Studies in Romanticism* 8 (1969), pp. 95–108.

de Man, Paul, 'Autobiography as De-facement', *Comparative Literature* 94, no. 5 (December 1979), pp. 919–30.

De Quincey, Thomas, *The Works of Thomas De Quincey [Confessions of an English Opium-Eater]*, ed. Grevel Lindop, vol. 2, The Pickering masters (London: Pickering & Chatto, 2000).

De Selincourt, Basil, *William Blake* (London: Duckworth, 1909).

DeBold, Richard C., and Russell C. Leaf, eds, *LSD, Man & Society* (Connecticut: Wesleyan Press, 1967).

Diamond, John, *Holism and Beyond: The Essence of Holistic Medicine* (Ridgefield: Enhancement Books, 2001).

—, *The Healing Power of Blake: A Distillation* (Bloomingdale: Creativity Press, 1998).

Easterlin, Nancy, *Wordsworth and the Question of 'Romantic Religion'* (Lewisburg: Bucknell University Press, 1996).

Ferguson, Francis, *Wordsworth, Language as Counter-Spirit* (New Haven: Yale University Press, 1977).

Fremantle, Anne Jackson, ed., *The Protestant Mystics* (Bordeaux, 1924).

Gadamer, Hans-Georg, *Truth and Method*. 2nd rev. edn (London: Sheed and Ward, 1989).

Gilchrist, Alexander, *Gilchrist on Blake: The Life of William Blake by Alexander Gilchrist*, ed. Richard Holmes (London: HarperCollins, 2005).

Gill, Stephen, *Wordsworth and the Victorians* (Oxford: Oxford University Press, 1998).

—, *William Wordsworth: A Life*, new edn (Oxford: Oxford Paperbacks, 1990).

Ginsberg, Allen, 'First manifesto to end the bringdown', in *The Marihuana Papers*, ed. David Solomon (New York: New American Library, 1968), pp. 230–48.

—, 'A Blake Experience', in *On the Poetry of Allen Ginsberg*, ed. Lewis Hyde (Ann Arbor: University of Michigan Press, 1984), pp. 120–30.

Hagstrum, Jean H., ' "The Wrath of the Lamb": A Study of William Blake's Conversions', in *From Sensibility to Romanticism. Essays Presented to Frederick A. Pottle*, eds, Harold Bloom and Frederick Whiley Hilles (New York: Oxford University Press, 1965).

Haney, David P., *William Wordsworth and the Hermeneutics of Incarnation* (University Park: Pennsylvania State University Press, 1993).

Happold, F. C., *Mysticism: A Study and an Anthology,* rev. edn (London: Penguin, 1970).

Hayden, John O., Review of *Wordsworth: The Sense of History* by Alan Liu, in *Nineteenth-Century Literature*, Vol. 45, No. 2 (Sep., 1990), pp. 245–49.

Hayter, Alethea, *Opium and the Romantic Imagination* (London: Faber, 1968).

Hickey, Alison, *Impure Conceits: Rhetoric and Ideology in Wordsworth's 'Excursion'* (Stanford, CA: Stanford University Press, 1997).

Hilton, Nelson, *Literal Imagination: Blake's Vision of Words* (Berkeley: California University Press, 1983).

Holstein, Michael E., ' "An Apocalypse of the World Within": Autobiographical Exegesis in De Quincey's Confessions of an English Opium-Eater (1822)', in *Prose Studies* 2, no. 2 (1979), pp. 88–102.

Hopps, Gavin, and Jane Stabler, eds, *Romanticism and Religion from William Cowper to Wallace Stevens* (Aldershot: Ashgate, 2006).

Hudson, T. P., A. P. Baggs, and H. M. Warne, 'British History Online: Felpham' (2003) <http://www.british-history.ac.uk/report.aspx?compid=22943> [accessed 16 July 2008].

Huxley, Aldous, *The Doors of Perception and Heaven and Hell* (London: Vintage, 2004).

Huxley, Laura Archera, *This Timeless Moment: A Personal View of Aldous Huxley* (London: Chatto & Windus, 1969).

Hyde, Lewis, ed., *On the Poetry of Allen Ginsberg* (Ann Arbor: University of Michigan Press, 1984).

Jacobs, Alan, ed., *Poetry for the Spirit: Poems of Universal Wisdom and Beauty* (London: Watkins, 2002).

James, William, *Varieties of Religious Experience: A Study in Human Nature* (London: Routledge, 2002).

Jay, Mike, *Artificial Paradises* (London: Penguin Books Ltd., 1999).

Jenkins, Keith, *On 'What Is History?': From Carr and Elton to Rorty and White* (London: Routledge, 1995).

—, *Re-Thinking History*, rev. edn (London: Routledge Classics, 2003).

Jordan, G. Ray, 'LSD and Mystical Experiences', *Journal of Bible and Religion* 31, no. 2 (1963), pp. 114–23.

Katz, Steven T., *Mysticism and Philosophical Analysis* (London: Sheldon Press, 1978).

Kermode, Frank, *The Genesis of Secrecy: On the Interpretation of Narrative* (Cambridge, MA: Harvard University Press, 1979).

—, *The Sense of an Ending: Studies in the Theory of Fiction*, new edn (Oxford: Oxford University Press, 2000).

Kincaid, James R., *Annoying the Victorians* (New York: Routledge, 1995).

Klonsky, Milton, *William Blake: The Seer and His Visions* (London: Orbis Pub, 1977).

Kornfield, Jack, *A Path with Heart*, rev. and updated edn (London: Rider & Co, 2002).

Kripal, Jeffrey J., *Roads of Excess, Palaces of Wisdom: Eroticism and Reflexivity in the Study of Mysticism* (Chicago: University of Chicago Press, 2002).

Kuhn, Thomas S., *The Structure of Scientific Revolutions* (Chicago: University of Chicago Press, 1962).

Lister, Raymond, *The Paintings of William Blake* (Cambridge: Cambridge University Press, 1986).

Liu, Alan, *The Laws of Cool: Knowledge Work and the Culture of Information* (Chicago: Chicago University Press, 2004).

—, *Wordsworth, the Sense of History* (Stanford, CA: Stanford University Press, 1989).

Marler, Penny Long, and C. Kirk Hadaway, '"Being Religious" or "Being Spiritual" in America: A Zero-Sum Proposition?',

Journal for the Scientific Study of Religion 41, no. 2 (2002), pp. 289–300.

Masters, Robert, and Jean Houston, *The Varieties of Psychedelic Experience* (Rochester: Park Street Press, 2000).

McGann, Jerome J., *The Poetics of Sensibility: A Revolution in Literary Style* (Oxford: Clarendon, 1996).

Merkur, Dan, *The Mystery of Manna: The Psychedelic Sacrament of the Bible* (Rochester: Park Street Press, 2000).

Nichols, Ashton, *The Poetics of Epiphany* (Alabama: University of Alabama Press, 1987).

Nicholson, D. H. S., and A. H. E. Lee, eds, *The Oxford Book of English Mystical Verse* (Oxford: Clarendon Press, 1917).

Nurmi, Martin Karl, *Blake's Marriage of Heaven and Hell: A Critical Study* (Ohio: Kent, 1957).

Reed, Mark L., *Wordsworth: The Chronology of the Middle Years 1800–1815* (Cambridge, MA: Harvard University Press, 1975).

Rix, Robert, *William Blake and the Cultures of Radical Christianity* (Aldershot: Ashgate, 2007).

Roberts, Daniel Sanjiv, '"Mix(ing) a Little with Alien Natures": Biblical Orientalism in De Quincey', in *Thomas De Quincey: New Theoretical and Critical Directions*, eds, Robert Morrison and Daniel Sanjiv Roberts (London: Routledge, 2008), pp. 19–43.

Roberts, Jonathan, 'St Paul's Gifts to Blake's Aesthetic', *The Glass* 15 (2003), pp. 8–18.

—, 'De Quincey's uses of the Bible', in *Religion, Literature and the Imagination*, eds, Mark Knight and Louise Lee (London: Continuum, 2009), pp. 123–39.

—, 'Wordsworth's Apocalypse', *Literature and Theology* 20, no. 4 (2006), pp. 361–78.

Robinson, Henry Crabb, *Diary, Reminiscences, and Correspondence*, ed. Thomas Sadler, vol. 1, 3 vols., 2nd edn (London: Macmillan & Co., 1869).

Rorty, Richard, *Contingency, Irony, and Solidarity* (Cambridge: Cambridge University Press, 1989).

Roston, Murray, *Prophet and Poet: The Bible and the Growth of Romanticism* (London: Faber & Faber, 1965).

Rowland, Christopher, *Blake and the Bible* (New Haven: Yale University Press, 2010).

Ryan, Robert M., *The Romantic Reformation: Religious Politics in English Literature, 1789–1824* (Cambridge: Cambridge University Press, 1997).

Rzepka, Charles J., *Sacramental Commodities: Gift, Text, and the Sublime in De Quincey* (Amherst: University of Massachusetts Press, 1995).

Schleiermacher, Friedrich, *On Religion* (Cambridge: Cambridge University Press, 1988).

Seidlitz, Larry, Alexis D. Abernethy, Paul R. Duberstein, James S. Evinger, Theresa H. Chang, and Bar'Bara L. Lewis, 'Development of the Spiritual Transcendence Index', *Journal for the Scientific Study of Religion* 41, no. 3 (September 2002), pp. 439–53.

Smith, Huston, *Cleansing the Doors of Perception: The Religious Significance of Entheogenic Plants and Chemicals* (New York: Jeremy P. Tarcher/Putnam, 2000).

Solomon, David, ed., *The Marihuana Papers* (New American Library, 1968).

Spurgeon, Caroline Frances Eleanor, *Mysticism in English Literature* (Cambridge: Cambridge University Press, 1913).

Stace, W. T., *Mysticism and Philosophy* (London: Macmillan, 1961).

Stevens, Jay, *Storming Heaven: LSD and the American Dream* (New York: Grove Press, 1987).

Trevor, John, *My Quest for God* ('Labour Prophet' Office: London, 1897).

Traherne, Thomas, *Centuries of Meditations* (New York: Cosimo, 2007).

Ulmer, William A., *The Christian Wordsworth, 1798–1805* (Albany: State University of New York Press, 2001).

Underhill, Evelyn, *Mysticism. A Study in the Nature and Development of Man's Spiritual Consciousness* (London: Methuen, 1911).

Van Fraassen, Bas C., *The Empirical Stance* (New Haven: Yale University Press, 2002).

Watson, J. R., *Wordsworth's Vital Soul: The Sacred and Profane in Wordsworth's Poetry* (London: Macmillan, 1982).

Wells, David, *A Study of William Blake's Letters* (Tübingen: Stauffenburg-Verlag, 1987).

Westbrook, Deeanne, *Wordsworth's Biblical Ghosts* (New York: Palgrave, 2001).

Wittgenstein, Ludwig, *Philosophical Investigations: The German Text with a Revised English Translation*, 3rd edn (Oxford: Blackwell, 2001).

Wordsworth, Dorothy, *The Grasmere and Alfoxden Journals*, ed. Pamela Woof (Oxford: Oxford University Press, 2008).

Wordsworth, Jonathan, *William Wordsworth: The Pedlar. Tintern Abbey. The Two-Part Prelude* (Cambridge: Cambridge University Press, 1985).

Wordsworth, William, *Letters of William Wordsworth: A New Selection*, ed. Alan Geoffrey Hill (Oxford: Clarendon Press, 1984).

—, *The Excursion*, ed. Sally Bushell, James Butler, and Michael C Jaye (Ithaca, NY: Cornell University Press, 2008).

—, *The Prose Works of William Wordsworth*, eds, W. J. B. Owen and Jane Worthington Smyser, 3 vols (Oxford: Clarendon Press, 1974).

Wright, Julia M., *Blake, Nationalism, and the Politics of Alienation* (Athens, Ohio: Ohio University Press, 2004).

Zaehner, R. C., *Mysticism Sacred and Profane* (Oxford: Clarendon Press, 1957).

—, *Drugs, Mysticism and Make-Believe* (London: Collins, 1972).

Zinnbauer, Brian J., Kenneth I. Pargament, Brenda Cole, Mark S. Rye, Eric M. Butter, Timothy G. Belavich, et al., 'Religion and Spirituality: Unfuzzying the Fuzzy', *Journal for the Scientific Study of Religion* 36, no. 4 (1997), pp. 549–64.

INDEX

1 Corinthians 101

Acts 79
Adams, Hazard 53
Altizer, Thomas 53, 75, 79
Ault, Donald 80
Autobiography 26, 66

Barth, J. Robert 52
Bible, the 54, 75, 76, 77
Biography 30, 37, 66
Blake, Catherine 7, 10, 11
Blake, William, works of
  'Ah, Sun-flower' 62
  'Jacob's Ladder' 90
  Jerusalem 97, 101, 102
  'Landscape near
    Felpham' 7–9, 33–7
  'The Little Girl Lost' 62
  *The Marriage of Heaven
    and Hell* 42
  Milton 9
  'The Sea of Time and
    Space' 90
  'The Sick Rose' 62
  'To my friend Butts' 4,
    7–15, 88
  *Songs of Innocence and of
    Experience* 65, 96
  A Vision of the Last
    Judgment 90
Boon, Marcus 58
Butts, Mrs 12, 15
Butts, Thomas 9, 12, 15, 89

Coleridge, Samuel Taylor 56,
  57, 65, 73

Damon, S. Foster 52
Damrosch Jr., Leopold 53,
  69, 80
Davie, Grace 82, 87
Davies, J. G. 52, 75
de Man, Paul 27
De Quincey, Thomas 55–7,
  65, 72, 73, 90, 103

Easterlin, Nancy 85–7
Enlightenment, the xii, 99
Exodus 55
Ezekiel 77, 78, 80, 91

Fawcett, Joseph 15–19, 25, 29
Felpham 5, 7, 9, 10, 12, 30,
  31, 35, 36, 52, 65, 89
Fenwick, Isabella 28
Foundationalism 5
French Revolution, the 16, 92

Gadamer, Hans-Georg xi
Ginsberg, Allan 58, 61–5

Haney, David P. 75
Happold, F. C. 52, 54
Harvard University 58
Hawkshead 43, 45, 46
Hayley, William 7, 11
Hayter, Alethea 57
Hermeneutical circle 2

Hermeneutics xi–xiii
Hickey, Alison 90, 92
Hilton, Nelson 100
Holstein, Michael E. 72, 73
Huxley, Aldous 42, 54, 58, 60, 71

Isaiah 76, 78, 80, 91

Jackson, Ruth 17, 28
James, William 49–51, 53, 62, 71
Jesus 11, 80, 102
John of Patmos 78–80, 90
John of the Cross 54
John, Gospel of 79
Jordan, G. Ray 65

Kornfield, Jack 102
'Kubla Khan' 66

Leary, Timothy 58
Lichtenstein, Roy 37
Lister, Raymond 34
LSD 43, 55, 57, 58
Luff, Mr. 28–9

Mayhew, Christopher 61, 72
Merkur, Dan 54, 55
Mescaline 43, 54
Mill, John Stuart 64

Native American Church 55
New Jerusalem 4, 77, 92

Osmond, Humphrey 58

Panorama 72
Paul the apostle 11, 78–80, 101
Psilocybin 57

Religious experience 2, 3, 26, 28, 38
Revelation 77–9, 93
Robinson, Henry Crabb 52
Rorty, Richard 97–100

Schleiermacher, Friedrich 85
Scolfield, John 9
Seurat, Georges-Pierre 37
Simplon Pass 28
Smith, Huston 70, 72
Solitary, the 15, 19, 25, 27–9, 56, 77, 79, 90–3, 102
Stace, W. T. 49, 53
Stanford University 58

Traherne, Thomas 45, 61, 90
Trevor, J. 50, 51, 53, 61, 85
Triangulation 34, 37

Ulmer, William A. 52
Underhill, Evelyn 49, 51, 53

Watson, J. R. 91
Wells, David 53
Westbrook, Deanne 75, 103
Westmoreland 17
White, Hayden 30
Wittgenstein, Ludwig 97, 98
Wordsworth, Catherine 28, 56
Wordsworth, Dorothy 28
Wordsworth, Jonathan 52
Wordsworth, Thomas 28
Wordsworth, William, works of
    Essays upon Epitaphs 99
    Excursion, The 4, 15–23, 25, 27–9, 56, 57, 65, 74, 77, 79, 91, 102
    Lyrical Ballads 96
    Prelude, The 25, 27, 28, 30

'Tintern Abbey' 27, 64, 74, 100

'Vaudracour and Julia' 28

Zaehner, R. C. 70, 71, 72, 74

Zinnbauer, B. J. 82, 83, 84, 85